THE FLOWER VASE

THE FLOWER VASE

Sarah C. Edgarton Mayo

Edited with an Introduction by
Gaia Elana McCune

WHITLOCK PUBLISHING
Alfred, NY

Original publication date:
The Flower Vase by Sarah Carter Edgarton Mayo, 1844

First Whitlock Publishing edition 2025

Whitlock Publishing
Alfred, New York

Editorial matter © Gaia Elana McCune

ISBN: 978-1-943115-58-7

Cover art courtesy of Wikimedia Commons
Image: Chrysanthemum by William Morris

TABLE OF CONTENTS

INTRODUCTION i

BIOGRAPHY v

TIMELINE OF VICTORIAN FLORIOGRAPHY vii

THE FLOWER VASE 1

SUGGESTED READING 161

Introduction

For thousands of years, gifting flowers has remained one of the most universally recognized gestures of affection, celebration, and sympathy. Flowers can convey emotions when words may not suffice: bouquets of roses on Valentine's Day, poinsettias for Christmas, or a spray of wildflowers to brighten a room. The tradition of gifting flowers is less concerned with the flower itself, but instead the symbolism it carries—the message construed through each bud and petal. People often assign meaning to certain flowers. Take the concept of a birth flower, for example; chosen in part for their seasonal significance, the blooms are meant to correlate to the general idea of a person born in that month. Someone born in April might receive a bouquet of daisies on their birthday, emblematic of innocence and purity. A November birthday might receive chrysanthemums, symbolizing life and rebirth. These monthly associations echo a much older tradition: the Victorian language of flowers, also known as floriography, a complex system for communicating emotion through the careful crafting of bouquets and floral arrangements.

To understand the Victorian obsession with floriography, it is important to understand the ancestry of the craft. Many of the unique meanings connected to flowers stem, in large part, from the symbolism of color. White flowers for purity, red for passion, pink for romance—these associations are not necessarily species-specific. However, when color symbolism is combined with factors such as time of bloom, fragrance, and unique growth habits, flowers can exude far more significance beyond the color of their petals. Different cultures also prescribe different meanings—a flower may have evoked vastly different sentiments from a Victorian lady than it would from a Japanese noblewoman.

Victorian floriography can be traced back to the Turkish tradition sélam, a sort of "language of objects" invented by women of harems to communicate in secret with their lovers. However, sélam was not necessarily a symbolic language, and it did not utilize flowers. First introduced to French audiences by letters written by Lady Mary Wortley Montagu and Seigneur Aubry de la Mottraye, sélam consisted of messages comprised of groups of objects bound in handkerchiefs. The objects themselves were insignificant, as they were meant to imply a rhyme or phrase. For example, if sélam were being utilized in English, a piece of rope might be used to imply a rhyming word such as "hope," which would then be inferred to indicate a longer sentiment such as "please give me hope." Despite the elaborate style and rules, sélam was viewed as more of a pastime or game than a legitimate way to communicate.

From this Turkish game, European travelers adapted the idea of sélam to include objects that were typically seen as having romantic connotations in their culture. Europeans westernized the tradition by combining their connections of flowers as romantic objects and the Eastern traditions of courtship to form the beginnings of Victorian floriography.

While the notion of a "language of flowers" took hold, Europeans still lacked a comprehensive way to "learn" the language. The invention of the flower book solved this problem; originating in France, these books drew inspiration from previous publications such as *La guirlande de Julie*, a book of flower poems and illustrations. Published first in 1641 as a birthday gift from the Marquis de Montausier for his fiancée, new editions appeared in 1784 and again in 1818. During the years between these two editions, the French aristocracy latched onto the idea of gifting small, almanac-style books containing floral illustrations and poetry. By the nineteenth century, this tradition trickled down from the gentility to lower classes, with flower books becoming a popular and fashionable gift.

One of the key features of these flower books is their "vocabularies," or catalog of different flower species and their assigned meanings. These vocabularies first appeared in the late 18th century as handwritten manuscripts, but eventually became a staple in flower books. Author B. Delachénaye, writer of one of the earliest French flower books, *Abécédaire de Flore ou langage des fleurs* (1810), included a vocabulary compiled from multiple of these handwritten lists, while expressing his dissatisfaction with the varying definitions across differing lists. Delachénaye's vocabulary pulled much of its meaning from sound—using the length or sharpness of vowels and consonants of the flower's name to substitute for written words. His attempt to create a sort of floral "alphabet" felt overcomplicated to many readers, who preferred vocabularies associated with feelings, instead of an authoritative and complex system of spelling.

Perhaps the most influential vocabulary of floral meanings was included in the French author Charlotte de Latour's book *Le langage des fleurs*. Published in 1819, Latour's book is often credited with the proliferation of flower books from France to countries such as England and America. Latour, widely believed by 19th-century scholars to be an aristocratic man writing under a female pseudonym, stood out among other floriography authors because of the unique seasonal organization and detailed descriptions of the flowers, noting each bloom's appearance and growth at length before explaining its meaning in the floriography language. Latour also included much more poetry and poetic verse in her book, using anecdotes to complement the definitions and engage readers.

The success of Latour's book not only encouraged other French authors but also inspired English authors to begin writing their own floriography books. However, contention between English modesty and loose French morality caused some authors to alter the meanings of certain flowers. Henry Phillips, author of one of the first English floriography books titled *Floral Emblems* (1825), directly acknowledges Latour's work, but also alludes to his mistrust of the French author, as he writes that he wishes to avoid any double-entendre or offensive allusion. Unlike the French books of the past, Phillips dedicates his book to "the Poets and Painters of Great Britain," catering to intellectuals, seemingly in an attempt to erase the suggestive origins of floriography. Unfortunately, Phillips' book failed to capture upper-class female readers and did not sell particularly well. Ironically, the first English flower book that garnered commercial success was Frederic Shoberl's *The Language of Flowers; With Illustrative Poetry* (1834), a translation of Latour's *Le langage des fleurs*. Shoberl edited Latour's book only slightly, substituting English plants in place of French ones within the main text; however, he copied Latour's floral vocabulary directly.

After Shoberl's publication, new flower books appeared frequently in England, often intended for the gift-book market. Popular books were published in many different editions and stayed in print for decades. Later titles began including various fortune-telling games, the most popular of which was called the Dial of Flowers, as seen in John Henry Ingram's *Flora Symbolica* (1869). The inclusion of these games become popular and reinvigorated floriography for new English readers even as the practice began to wane in France by the 1880s.

Floriography in America began with naturalists; the trend went hand-in-hand the popularity of nature literature during the early nineteenth century. The first appearance of flower books in America came from a French-born man of Turkish ancestry named Constantine Samuel Rafinesque. A scientific and eccentric man, he published *Medical Flora* in 1828, a work composed of short publications that had appeared in various periodicals in years prior. However, contrasting the heavily male-dominated market of Europe, American flower books were often penned by female authors. This trend inspired the association between floriography and upward class mobility for female writers. Although Rafinesque's work was the first, the genre would not become popular until the following year when Elizabeth Gamble Wirt published *Flora's Dictionary* in 1829. Wirt published her book under the moniker "A Lady" and found huge success, eventually seeing multiple editions go to print. Although the 1830s saw the rise of flower books in America, the genre truly hit its peak in the 1840s and 50s, with editions featuring ornate illustrations, intricate bindings, and lofty titles.

As flower books grew in popularity, additional flower-centric books began rising in the market as well, with anthologies of flower poetry finding market success. Often, flower books and poetic anthologies were combined in collections consisting of brief entries of a flower's meaning or classification, followed by a poem bolstering the sentiment. One of the earliest versions of these anthologies was Sarah Edgarton Mayo's *The Flower Vase* (1844). Although *The Flower Vase* focused on floral poetry, the was not Mayo's first foray into floriography—one of Mayo's earlier publications, *The Floral Fortune Teller*, combined floriography and popular American fortune-telling books. The book would provide short, simple poems that correspond with different flowers. A reader could ask one of five questions, then choose a flower from a bouquet; the color of the flower would indicate a specific line of poetry to answer the original question.

Like most trends, floriography fell out of fashion after the nineteenth century in England and America as quickly as it had caught on due to rising political conflicts, threats of war, and industrial advances. Contemporary audiences often tend to over-dramatize the art of floriography, indulging in an idealized Victorian fantasy and mistakenly describing the language as a consistent method of communication across decades. However, the history of the language of flowers is a fragmented, fleeting trend that was more of a fancy for those who owned flower books. While twenty-first century books published about the "Victorian language of flowers" are entertaining, their popularity does not directly reflect the reality of floriography's significance in the Victorian era.

Biography of Sarah C. Edgarton Mayo

Born to Joseph Edgarton and his second wife Mehitable Whitcomb on March 17th, 1819, in Shirley, Massachusetts, Sarah Carter Edgarton Mayo was the tenth of fifteen children. Despite the staggering number of children, the family was financially comfortable, and Sarah was able to attend and excel at her district school. Under the name Sarah C. Edgarton, she submitted many poems and essays for publication at the young age of sixteen in an attempt to contribute to her family's finances. At age seventeen, Sarah joined the Universalist church of her parents and was able to maintain a comfortable station as a writer, finding a market for her work with a popular New England women's periodical in Boston, the Universalist and Ladies' Repository. The magazine focused on bettering its reader's moral virtue and literary knowledge, leading Mayo to focus on topics emphasizing ethical sentiments and virtuous actions. In the late 1830s, Mayo also found success publishing didactic children's tales; she published *The Palfreys* and *Ellen Clifford; or, The Genius of Reform* both in 1838, with the former publication aimed at grade school children, and the latter geared towards adolescents.

In 1839, Mayo was invited to become an associate editor of the Universalist, and she maintained that position until 1842. When her editorship was announced in the publication, she pledged to dedicate her time to bettering female education and literary interest, and hoped to encourage readers to maintain disciplined lifestyles revolving around reading, meditation, and domestic satisfaction. Starting in 1840, Mayo also began editing the popular Universalist annual gift publication named *The Rose of Sharon: A Religious Souvenir.*

Mayo would go on to publish two collections of poetry of her own, *Spring Flowers* in 1840 and *The Poetry of Woman* in 1841. The first of the flower books she published was *The Flower Vase*, first published in 1843 and eventually going through many editions both in America and England. She followed her first floriography book publication with *Fables of Flora* in 1844, a collection of fables written by herself and popular English poet John Langhorne.

In 1846, Mayo published *The Floral Fortune Teller*, a book detailing an elaborate game of flowers and poetry. *The Floral Fortune Teller* also saw many editions, and the funds she made from those publications allowed her to financially support her family financially and fund the education of her younger brother John at Harvard.

In 1846, Sarah married Amory Dwight Mayo, a Universalist clergyman and author. After marriage, the couple moved to Gloucester, Massachusetts where Sarah Mayo spent the last two years of her life. During those years, Mayo worked on a small number of poems for the *Rose*, a literary magazine she intended to publish with her brother. This endeavor was abandoned, however, with her brother John's unexpected death in October of 1847. Mayo would attempt to write more after the loss but became discouraged and destroyed all but a few pieces of the literature of her late life. She spent her last months caring for her daughter, born in September of 1847. Sarah of an illness less than a year later in July of 1848.

This edition of Mayo's book provides contemporary readers with a glimpse into the world of Victorian floriography, using poetry and floral classification to highlight the meanings behind each flower or plant included. With poems written by multiple authors, some by Mayo herself, the collection is an interesting glimpse in the history behind the lost language, providing a window into a past and preserving the work of a brilliant and talented American woman.

A Timeline of Victorian Floriography

1810 Author B. Delachénaye publishes his flower book *Abécédaire de Flore ou langage des fleurs*, including a "vocabulary" of flowers and their meanings.

1819 French author Charlotte de Latour publishes *Le langage des fleurs*, which popularized the "language of flowers" on a larger scale in France with its unique organization and including more than simple lists of flowers.

1825 Henry Phillips publishes *Floral Emblems* through English publishing company Saunders and Otley, crediting French author Charlotte de Latour for her work but still denouncing potential French "immodesty."

1828 Constantine Samuel Rafinesque publishes *Medical Flora* in America, a work composed of short publications that had appeared in various periodicals in years prior. This book mainly focused on scientific classification, and did not sell particularly well.

1829 Elizabeth Gamble Wirt publishes *Flora's Dictionary* under the moniker "A Lady," finding huge success and seeing multiple editions go to print.

1831 A second edition of Phillips *Floral Emblems* is published, despite low popularity of the first edition.

1834 Frederic Shoberl publishes *The Language of Flowers; With Illustrative Poetry*, a slightly edited translation of Latour's *Le langage des fleurs*. Shoberl substituted French plants with those more commonly seen in England.

1836 Robert Tyas publishes *The Sentiment of Flowers; or, Language of Flora*, which quickly becomes the most profitable English book on the language of flowers.

1839 Tyas's book *The Sentiment of Flowers; or, Language of Flora* reaches 6,000 copies sold.

1844 Sarah C. Edgarton Mayo publishes *The Flower Vase*.

1869 John Henry Ingram's *Flora Symbolica* is published, which includes a fortune-telling game, called the Dial of Flowers, helping to briefly reinvigorate the floriography trend.

1880s Floriography declines in popularity greatly as political tensions begin growing in France and England, and the focus of the world begins transitioning heavily towards industrialization.

The Flower Vase

The heart is Love's rich vase, wherein are cast
Bright hopes, like flowers, too fair and frail to last;
But while they bloom, oh be their perfume shed
In clouds of sweetness, dear one, round thy head.

THE FLOWER VASE;
CONTAINING
THE LANGUAGE OF FLOWERS
AND
THEIR POETIC SENTIMENTS.

BY MISS S. C. EDGARTON.

'Love hath its symbols; hence, in far Cathay,
And where the arrowy Tigris rolls his wave,
The fragrant reeds and woods, whose bending trunks
Weep precious balms; and on those palmy fields
Where erst the majesty of Persia fell,
The words of passion find an utterance thus,
And all its nameless feelings stand revealed
By emblems gathered from the grove and rill.
Methinks our land, as fair and green as these,
Might furnish matter, in its mossy glades
And fern-invested rills, where thought should rove
And young imagination sport as free.'

J. F. Hollings.

LOWELL:
POWERS AND BAGLEY.
BOSTON: B. B. MUSSEY, CORNHILL.
1844.

Entered according to Act of Congress, in the year 1843,
By A. C. Bagley,
In the Clerk's Office of the District Court of the District of
Massachusetts.

BOSTON:
Samuel N. Dickinson, Printer,
Washington Street.

PREFACE.

This little volume is put forth, not for its originality of design or arrangement, but because it embraces the language and poetic sentiments of flowers in a smaller and less expensive form than any similar work hitherto before the public.

The poetic sentiments are chiefly original; those that have been selected are usually from sources not attainable to the mass of readers, and will, we think, be as new as they are appropriate. The language of the flowers is, in most cases, that which has been established by popular acceptance. Where authorities differ, we have followed our own taste.

The prose descriptions are necessarily brief and simple. The botanic name and classification are given, as a reference to more elaborate and scientific description in works devoted to floral

analyzation. 'Flora's Interpreter,'—the best of the flower books,—has been our guide in this; but, though imitating, we have not copied.

The study of flowers is so interesting, and their connection with poetry so natural, that it is hardly necessary to commend any work of this class to the notice of the cultivators or the lovers of flowers. We only ask for ours, that it may have its day with the rest.

SEPTEMBER 1, 1843.

DEDICATION.

'T is said that in gorgeous Eastern climes,
Where folks are too idle for stringing rhymes,
When a lover would send to his lady a token
Of love, which in words may not be spoken,
He hies away to the garden bowers,
And culls a boquet of the fairest flowers;
Which, woven together of magic art,
Are the language of love to the maiden's heart!

No tale of passion have I to breathe;
Yet, gentle reader, I fain would wreathe
A floral garland, whose leaves shall be
Emblems and tokens of love to thee.
FLOWERS!—they bloom by the lowliest cot—
May they gladden, and brighten, and bless thy lot!

AMARANTH.

AMARANTHUS. *Class* 19. — *Order* 5.

Of this plant there are many species. Among the prettiest is the Coxcomb—flowers red, unfading.

Immortality.

Oh, not for the hue of thy roseate cheek,
Nor the dimpled rubies that smile and speak,
Oh, not for the flash of thy glowing eye,
Nor the eloquent sound of thy soft, low sigh,
Do I love thee, bright being of passion and grace!
'T is the SOUL, the sweet soul in thy beautiful face,
The spirit immortal, the charm that ne'er dies,
That from death and the gloom of the grave will arise;
It is *this* that enthrals me; and thou unto me
Art the embryo, only, of what thou shalt be;
For thy mortal shall die; but the beauty I love,
Hath an endless existence and progress above!

ANEMONE.

ANEMONE. *Class* 13. — *Order* 13. Wind-flower.

This plant is native to America, and is one of the earliest harbingers of Spring. The flowers are of various colors — blue, white, purple, etc.

Frailty.

LIFE'S frosts thou art too frail to bear,
And in its storms would perish;
A floweret Love alone should wear,
And on his bosom cherish.

Love, like a rock, should firmly stand,
And hang its shelter o'er thee;
While only zephyrs soft and bland,
Dispense their sweets before thee.

ASTER.

ASTER. *Class* 19. — *Order* 2. Starwort.

This is one of the most common of American wild flowers, and has almost every variety of color. The genus consists of more than one hundred species; of which none is prettier than the purple wood-aster, that blooms in September and October.

Beauty in retirement.

THOU, like a star-flower in the wood,
   Thy modest charms art hiding;
Content with humbly doing good,
   And in God's love abiding.

But though the world observes thee not,
   In one fond heart thou 'rt treasured;
And bright indeed must be the lot
   That shares a love unmeasured.

ACACIA.

ACACIA. *Class* 17. — *Order* 10.

Platonic Love.

Lo, others kneel before thy shrine
  With Passion's words of fire;
But better far such love as mine,
  That never feels desire.

To pray for thee at twilight hour,
  To dream of thee at night,
To link thy name with every flower—
  These make *my* love's delight.

And years may roll, and time may mar
  The beauty of thy brow,
But thou, however distant far,
  Wilt be as dear as now.

From Passion and its stains refined,
  My love is deep and pure;
Shall it not, born of heart and mind,
  As long as these endure?

APPLE BLOSSOM.

PYRUS. *Class* 12. — *Order* 5.

This is a blossom too well known to require description. Nothing, however, can be more delicious than the soft perfume shed by it upon the breezes of May. And then how like snow-flakes it falls over the green and dewy sward!

Fame speaks you great and good.

THY name is heard in crowds—
 They call thee good and great;
The brightness of the sunset clouds
 Seems showered upon thy fate.
Where'er thy pathway leads
 They strew it o'er with flowers—
Emblems of generous deeds
 Thy heart profusely showers;
Oh, good and great forever be—
 Worthy the praise they yield to thee!

ASH.

FRAXINUS. *Class* 21. — *Order* 2.

There are six varieties of the Ash native to our forests. It is a handsome as well as useful tree; and in Autumn wears a very gorgeous apparel.

Grandeur.

COSTLY the jewels that gleam on thy breast—
Beautiful maiden! say, art thou blest?
Rich are the robes that envelope thy form—
Beats there beneath them a heart that is warm?
Beautiful maiden! slaves wait thy command—
Leadest thou them with a lenient hand?
Grandeur is round thee, wherever thou art—
Oh say, is there brightness like this in thy heart?
If so, may no sorrows of mine ever dim
The joys that are mantling thy cup to its brim;
In the shade of my lot, I'll adore thee afar—
The worm on the earth may look up to the star!

ALYSSUM.

ALYSSUM. *Class* 15. — *Order* 1.

Worth beyond beauty.

THOU art not beautiful—ah, no!
  Not what the world calls fair;
No roses on a cheek of snow
  Beam through soft curling hair;
Thou art not beautiful; and yet
  Thy looks are full of grace;
The seal of wisdom, too, is set
  Upon thy modest face.

And better far such charms as these,
  Than those that fade with years;
Give me the beauty that can please
  When withered eld appears.
For time, that pales the rosiest cheek
  And tracks the smoothest brow,
Will leave *thy spirit* pure and meek,
  And beautiful as now.

BACHELOR'S BUTTON.

GOMPHRENA. *Class* 5. — *Order* 1.

This is the pretty Globe Amaranth, with the round, red, unfading blossoms. Commonly cultivated.

Hope in Misery.

THE cloud may be dark, but there's sunshine beyond it;
    The night may be o'er us, but morning is near;
The vale may be deep, but there's music around it,
    And hope, mid our anguish, bright hope is still here.

Still here, though the wing of dark sorrow is o'er us,
    Tho' bitterness dregs every cup that we drink;
With a smile in her eye, she glides ever before us
    To yield us support when we falter or sink.

Blessed hope! like a star on the darkness of ocean,
    Still gleam o'er the track where our destinies tend;
And guide our frail hearts from this sea of commotion,
    To havens of peace where our sorrows will end.

BALM.

MELISSA NEPETA. *Class* 14. — *Order* 1.

This species is commonly called Rose-balm, and is highly aromatic. It is known also by the name of Calamint. The flowers are red and blue, and disposed in heads or corymbs.

Sweets of Social Intercourse.

I HAVE best loved those hours when, 'mid a group
Of chosen friends, I gave frank utterance
To every thought, and won *theirs* in return.
With books around the fireside, or with flowers
When summer reigns, how freely gush and blend
True hearts in unison! To man how dear
His cheerful hearthstone when the day is o'er;
And woman—sure *her* heart was wholly made
For sweet communion at the social shrine.

BALM OF GILEAD.

POPULUS BALSAMIFERA. *Class* 21. — *Order* 13.

There are many species of the Poplar. The Balm of Gilead is distinguished for its resinous and aromatic buds, which are useful for vulnerary application.

I am cured.

My dream is o'er, my heart at rest;
No idle hopes its peace molest;
Never again will love of mine
Be cast, rejected, from thy shrine.

It is not pride that bids me wear
A quiet and untroubled air;
My smiles are no poor tricks of art—
They speak the sunshine of my heart.

Farewell! Pursue in peace thy way;
I care not where thy feet may stray;
No idle griefs my peace molest,
My love is o'er, my heart at rest.

BALSAM.

IMPATIENS. *Class* 5. — *Order* 1.

This flower is commonly called Touch-me-not. The wild species grows by the brook-sides, and bears an orange-colored flower.

Impatience.

I CANNOT, Will not longer brook
Thy cold delay, thy prudent look!
Dost love me? Share at once my fate,
Be it or bright or desolate!
I will abide no half-way love,
Nor wait for prudence ere I move;
One more repulse, and I depart!
Come now, or never, to my heart.

BARBERRY.

BERBERIS. *Class* 6. — *Order* 1.

This graceful wild shrub is well known. It forms handsome hedges, and is much esteemed for its fruit. It bears a pretty yellow flower.

Petulance.

THAT frown but ill becomes thy face;
That pout hath spoilt thy lips' sweet grace;
Those peevish tones disturb the ear
Accustomed thy *soft* notes to hear.
Have I offended? Gently chide,
And I thine anger will abide;
Will kneel repentant at thy feet,
Until my pardon is complete.
Say, dost thou not this mood regret?
'Thou dost! Forgive, then, and forget.

BAY LEAF.

LAURUS. *Class* 9. — *Order* 1.

The Greek fable relates that Daphne was transformed into the Bay tree, and that Apollo, her lover, crowned his head with the leaves.

I change but in dying.

THOUGH fate ordains that we must part,
   And each fond tie doth sever,
Yet still thou reignest in my heart,
   To be dethronéd never!

Thy resting-place it still shall be,
   Should grief or care assail thee;
And when thy summer-friends all flee,
   This refuge ne'er shall fail thee.

Thy memory, fondly there enshrined,
   The dews of thought shall nourish;
And from the dross of earth refined,
   The plant of love shall flourish.

C. A. FILLEBROWN.

BIRCH.

BETULA. *Class* 20. — *Order* 13.

There are many varieties of the Birch, and all of them are graceful. Schoolboys consider the bark of the Spicy Birch a great treat.

Gracefulness.

LIKE the foam on the wave floating down to the sea,
Like the zephyr that flits o'er the grain-covered lea,
Like the soft fleecy cloud o'er the face of the moon,
Like the sail of a bird on the still air of noon,
So graceful, and airy, and gentle art thou,
With thy curls floating free o'er thy radiant brow!
So fairy-like moveth thy foot o'er the flowers,
They look up and exclaim—'T was the step of the Hours!'

BINDWEED.

CONVOLVULUS. *Class* 5. — *Order* 1.

This is a very pretty wild vine, with delicate pink flowers. There are eight species native to America.

Humility.

LIKE thy Saviour, maid, thou art,
Humble, lowly, meek of heart;
Fairest of the flowers of earth,
Yet unconscious of thy worth.

Ever thus pursue thy way,
Ever thus thy Lord obey;
Dearest of all charms to me
Is thy sweet humility.

BLUE BELL.

CAMPANULA. *Class* 5. — *Order* 1.

Six species of this flower are native to America. They are all beautiful, having blue or white nodding flowers.

Constancy.

THEY bid me forget him! as if I could tear
From my heart the dear image so long cherished there!
Like a rose in the wilderness, blooming and free,
Like a fount in the desert that love is to me!

I brood o'er my thoughts in the stillness of night;
I cannot forget him—*would* not, if I might!
'T is the star that illumines my desolate way,
And gives it the glory and brightness of day.

C. A. FILLEBROWN.

BOX.

BUXUS. *Class* 21. — *Order* 4.

There are two kinds of Box,—the Arborescent, which is twelve or sixteen feet high; and the Dwarf, which is used as a border for flower-beds.

Stoicism.

I NE'ER will weep again!
I will meet fate with an unblenching eye;
For better far in proud contempt to die,
    Than idly talk of pain.

Can I not bear *all things?*
Who talks of weakness to a soul like mine?
Love, hope, pity, sorrow I resign,
    And all that fortune brings.

In lonely strength I stand,
Unmoved though earthquakes open at my feet;
Though storms of malice on my bosom beat,
    I can their rage withstand.

BROOME.

GENISTA. *Class* 17. — *Order* 10.

Dyer's Broome bears a yellow flower, and blossoms in August. There are two other varieties, violet and white flowering.

Neatness.

I LOVE to see thy gentle hand
   Dispose, with modest grace,
The household things around thy home,
   And 'each thing in its place.'

And then thy own trim, modest form
   Is always neatly clad;
Thou sure wilt make the tidiest wife
   That ever husband had'

No costly splendors needest thou,
   To make thy home look bright;
For neatness on the humblest spot
   Can shed a sunny light.

BURDOCK.

ARCTIUM. *Class* 18. — *Order* 1.

This is known by its coarse, broad leaf, and round, bur-like blossom. Nurses know how to appreciate its value in alleviating pain.

Importunity.

Of thy teasings and pleadings
 I'm heartily sick;
I'm sure if I loved thee
 I'd tell thee so quick.

What use or advantage
 In wooing like this?
When a woman says '*No!*'
 Do you think she means '*Yes?*'

The longer thou suest
 The colder I grow;
There-take my last answer;
 Canst hear it? 'T is—No!

CALLA.

ARUM. *Class* 20. — *Order* 13.

This is a native of Ethiopia, and is much esteemed for its beautiful snow-white calyx, and broad green leaves.

Feminine Modesty.

THE blue bell by the meadow rill
   Is not more fair than thou,
With thy downcast and thoughtful eye,
   Thy pure and gentle brow.

All sweet and holy dreams seem blent
   Within thy maiden heart;
How delicate in every look,
   In every thought thou art!

The blush so frequent on thy cheek
   Thy meek and quiet air,
Thy low and gentle accents,—all
   Thy purity declare.

CHAMOMILE.

ANTHEMIS. *Class* 18. — *Order* 2.

This is a native of Europe-has a white or yellow flower, and is much loved for its fragrance.

Energy in Adversity.

ONWARD! Hath earth's ceaseless change
   Trampled on thy heart?
Faint not, for that restless range
   Soon will heal the smart.
Trust the future—time will prove
   Earth hath stronger, truer love.

Bless thy God, the heart is not
   An abandoned urn,
Where, all lonely and forgot,
   Dust and ashes mourn;
Bless Him, that his mercy brings
   Joy from out its withered things.

MRS. CASE.

CANDYTUFT.

IBERIS. *Class* 15. — *Order* 1.

This is a pretty garden-flower, bearing clusters of small white blossoms, and forms a very good border to a flower-garden.

Indifference

TAKE back thy flowers and *billet-doux*,
   Thy sonnets and thy rhymes;
To burn them all I've half resolved
   A dozen different times.

So much waste paper lying round—
   So many withered herbs—
I'm sure the very sight of them
   My quietude disturbs.

Thou knowest well I little care
   For gifts like these from thee;
'T is love alone gives worth to such—
   And thou hast none from me.

CARDINAL FLOWER.

LOBELIA. *Class* 5. — *Order* 1.

This is a beautiful flower, growing wild by our brooks and ditches. Flowers are a rich scarlet.

Distinction.

HEAVEN grant thee, friend, a high soft star to be,
Calm, still and bright, to trace thy way in heaven,
And shed thy light o'er life's tempestuous sea,
Where human hearts, like fragile barks, are driven
   'Mid rocks and hidden shoals ;
  A soul 'mid glorious souls-
A small pure star within the glittering band
That high above the clouds, undimmed and grand
   In placid beauty, rolls,
To herald on the weary to the land
Where all is rest and peace; to guide the way
   To heaven's unclouded day!

CARNATION.

DIANTHUS. *Class* 10. — *Order* 2.

This is a very rich and fragrant Pink, growing sometimes as large as a rose. It has a variety of colors-chiefly red and white.

Pride.

IT is not well amid thy race to move
And shut thy heart to sympathy and love.
It is not well to scorn inferior minds,
And pass them by as though they were but hinds.
Pride may become thee, as the veil a nun,
But ah! they love thee not, whom thou dost shun!
And days may come to thee when human love
Thou wilt desire all earthly things above;
And thou wilt mourn that in thy days of pride
Thou didst not win some true hearts to thy side;
Wilt mourn that now thy rank and wealth have flown,
Thou 'rt left to suffer and to die *alone!*

CATCHFLY.

SILENE. *Class* 10. — *Order* 3.

There are nearly one hundred species of this flower. That most common with us bears a pink blossom, and grows very tall.

A Snare.

OF winning words and tender looks,
   My artless friend, beware!
Along the path of human life
   Lurks many a fatal snare.

Trust seldom, and with much reserve;
   Few merit generous faith;
And should *guile* speak, oh give no heed
   To what the tempter saith.

I fear some treacherous snare is laid
   Along thy flowery way;
Oh, be thou cautious—smiles may cheat,
   And tender words betray!

CEDAR TREE.

JUNIPERUS. *Class* 20. — *Order* 12.

This tree is native to North America, and is one of our prettiest evergreens. The wood is considered quite valuable for many purposes of building, etc.

Spiritual Strength.

ONWARD, for the *truths* of *God!*
  Onward, for the *right!*
Firmly let the field be trod,
  In life's coming fight:
Heaven's own hand will lead thee on,
Guard thee till thy task is done!

Then will brighter, sweeter flowers
  Blossom round thy way,
Than e'er sprung in Hope's glad bowers
  In thine early day—
And the rolling years shall bring
Strength and healing on their wing.

MRS. CASE.

CHERRY BLOSSOM.

PRUNUS. *Class* 12. — *Order* 1.

There are a great many species of Cherry growing wild in our woods and glens. They all bear a pretty white blossom, of pleasant fragrance.

Spiritual Beauty.

I KNOW thou art not beautiful, nor art thou fortune's child,
Yet beameth ever from thine eye a spirit undefiled.
I know that genius never shed its radiance on thy brow,
Yet wert thou ever truthful, good, and kind as thou art now.

I know thy form was never cast in fashion's graceful mould,
Nor do I wish in fashion's throng thy presence to behold;
So long as Nature's nobleness has marked thee for her own,
I would not give thy soul-lit smile to share a monarch's throne!

MISS H. J. WOODMAN.

CHINA ASTER.

ASTER. *Class* 19. — *Order* 2.

A very extensive genus, of which we have many species in our woods, but none so beautiful as the cultivated *China Aster*.

Your sentiments meet with a return.

YES, I am thine! Upon thy bosom leaning,
   No grief hath power to damp my fervent bliss;
Nor can such love to thee be overweening—
   Thou art deserving all, and more than this!

Beloved, ne'er from thee one moment straying,
   My heart shall twine its roots upon thy truth;
All lighter loves than this are fast decaying,
   Lost in the dying years of sunny youth.

CHRYSANTHEMUM — YELLOW.

CHRYSANTHEMUM. *Class* 18. — *Order* 2.

This genus embraces the Ox-eyed Daisy, Feverfew, and two or three other species. The *Coronarium* is most cultivated in our gardens.

A heart left to desolation.

THE long, lone Future! It hath no gay dream,
   For nought can make it beautiful save thee;
Hope plants no garlands by life's shadowy stream,
   Nor are there blossoms on life's frost-hued tree.
And Fame, she may bring wreaths; I heed them not;
By all the world I pray to be forgot.

CINQUEFOIL.

POTENTILLA. *Class* 12. — *Order* 13.

There are twelve species of this little flower indigenous to America. The common Five-finger may be found in blossom along our road sides from April till the season of frosts.

Love, constant, but hopeless.

I CANNOT reproach thee! A malison rest
  On the word that would wound those kind feelings of thine!
Wert thou colder than snow on Monadanock's crest,
  The star of my love on thy spirit should shine.

Yet thou lovest me not as thou lovedst me of yore;
  A cloud hath arisen, and passed o'er the light;
It is well! May God bless thee, dear friend, evermore;
  So the sun but gild *thee*, I can welcome the night!

CLEMATIS.

CLEMATIS. *Class* 13. — *Order* 7. Virgin's Bower.

This is a very graceful vine, bearing white and pale blue flowers. It grows wild by our brooks, and is considerably cultivated in gardens.

Mental Excellence.

EXCELLING riches dwell within thy mind—
Strong, fervent thought, and eloquence refined;
Ideal beauty clusters round thy soul,
While deep within, the waves of feeling roll.
Religious fervor mingles with the grace
Of playful fancy, to illume thy face;
And sparkling wit with graver sense unites,
And fills thine eye with many changing lights.
Oh, beautiful, indeed, a mind like thine,
And well might angels bow at such a shrine;
But man, weak man, oft passes idly by,
To worship beauty that attracts the eye,
While mental grace, a charm that ne'er can fade,
Flies from the crowd, and dwells amid the shade.

COLUMBINE.

AQUILEGIA. *Class* 13. — *Order* 5.

This flower is well known. The wild Columbine of New England is of a bright red; those in our gardens are white, purple, pink, etc.

I cannot give thee up.

OH, blame me not that unto thee I pour
   The lavish treasures of unfathomed love;
'T is, dear one, but to plead with thee, no more
   To bid me crush what has its root above.
I shall die gently 'neath its shadowy spell,
And thou shalt know that *one* hath loved thee well.

Mistake me not; nor let one shadow fall
   Upon thy heart, already worn with pain;
Let me but love thee, serve thee; this is all;
   Grant me but this, and I am strong again;
Strong—for to love thee, though thou art not mine,
Is to my homeless heart an altar and a shrine.

CORN.

ZEA MAYS. *Class* 20. — *Order* 3.

There are several varieties of Corn, but the rich yellow ear is most in favor with New England farmers.

Riches.

If thou'lt be mine, no want or care
   Shall e'er disturb thy life;
Thy days shall all be bright and fair,
   With worldly blessings rife.

If thou'lt be mine, bright gems shall deck
   Thy snowy arms and breast,
And pearls shall cluster round thy neck,
   And on thy forehead rest.

If thou'lt be mine, what have I, love,
   That is not also thine?
Oh then my heart no longer prove,
   But say thou wilt be mine!

COWSLIP.

DODECATHEON. *Class* 5. — *Order* 1.

A very bright, beautiful yellow flower, growing in our meadows, and blossoming in May.

Native Grace.

    SHE grew in love. Around her infant home
        Life hung its summer hues, and very fair
    Was this wild earth to her. She learned to roam
        In artless radiance where the woodland air
    Showered trembling sweetness on the glancing streams,
    And stole its hue from sunset's golden beams.

    She twined the orchis in her hazel hair,
        And stole the violets from the brookside dell;
    The wilding race was her peculiar care,
        Her dearest music was the foxglove's bell,
    When the wild bee with his transparent wings
    Stirs the sweet air, and makes believe he sings.

COREOPSIS.

COREOPSIS. *Class* 19. — *Order* 3.

This is a bright yellow flower, much cultivated in modern gardens. It continues in bloom from June till autumn.

Always cheerful.

LOVELY thou art, ay, lovely;
   And sorrow shared with thee,
As if magician-changed, becomes
   A pleasure unto me.
Life's sky, though clothed with tempest clouds,
   Grows bright when thou art nigh,
And tears e'er turn to smiles beneath
   Thine angel-gifted eye.

                                MRS. SCOTT.

CORIANDER.

CORIANDRUM. *Class* 5. — *Order* 2.

This has a fragrant, spicy seed, formerly much esteemed by housewives and confectioners.

Concealed Merit.

NONE know thy goodness. Like the fragrant mint
Hid in the umbrage of some lowly glen,
Thy virtues lie concealed; and only love
In its deep research, can unlock the wealth
Of thy benignant soul, and bring to light
Its hidden jewels. The lone, suffering heart,
The humble poor, the sorrowing and forlorn,
These know thy worth. Oh, is not fame like this
Beyond the praises of a heartless world?

CYPRESS.

CYPRESSUS. *Class* 21. — *Order* 16.

Disappointed Hopes.

THEY came and went like shadows,
    The blessed dreams of youth,
And they left behind no impress
    Or record of their truth.
Then the future was all sunshine,
    In gorgeous robes arrayed;
But ever as I've reached it,
    Its sunshine turned to shade.

I've seen the colors fading
    From all that I could prize,
Like day's departing glories
    From out the sunset skies.
And full roughly I have ridden
    The stormy tide of life,
And long years have passed in struggling,
    In bitterness and strife.

T. B. THAYER.

DAHLIA.

DAHLIA. *Class* 19. — *Order* 2.

This is a Mexican plant, much cultivated by modern horticulturists. The flowers are of all colors, and very showy; growing often to the height of six or eight feet.

Elegance and Dignity.

It is worth much in this dull world of strife
And foolish vanity, to meet a heart
Serene and beautiful like thine! The praise
And selfish flattery of the heartless crowd,
Falls idly on thine ear, whilst thou, unmoved,
And with a lofty purpose in thy breast,
Retain'st thy elevation o'er the herd,
No less by that calm majesty of soul
Which shrinks from adulation, than by gifts
Of lofty intellect, and outward grace.
Thy form hath elegance that indicates
The beautiful refinement of thy thoughts;
And there is dignity in thy firm step,
That speaks a soul superior to the thrall
Of petty vanity and low-born pride.

DAISY.

BELLIS. *Class* 19. — *Order* 2.

This is a common European flower, but belongs to us only by cultivation. Colors, blue, pink and white.

Beauty and Innocence.

LOVELY thou art! ay, lovely,
  In spirit and in form;
A sunbeam glancing o'er life's tears,
  A rainbow through the storm;
A snow-drop 'mid earth's darker hues,
  Unwarmed by flattery's breath;
A harp-tone flung from cherub hands,
  Wringing out joy from death.

MRS. SCOTT.

DANDELION.

LEONTODON. *Class* 19. — *Order* 1.

This is a naturalized European flower, and one of the earliest that greets us on the return of Spring.

Coquetry.

I KNOW I share thy smiles with many,
    Yet still thy smiles are dear to me;
I know that I, far less than any,
    Call out thy spirit's witchery;
But yet I cannot help, when nigh thee,
    To seize upon each glance and tone,
To hoard them in my heart when by thee,
    And count them o'er whene'er alone.

But why, oh why, on all thus squander
    The treasures one alone can prize, —
Why let the looks at random wander,
    Which beam from those deluding eyes?
Those syren tones, so lightly spoken,
    Cause many a heart, I know, to thrill;
But mine, and only mine, till broken,
    In every pulse must answer still.

C. F. HOFFMAN.

DEW-PLANT.

MESEMBRYANTHEMUM. *Class* 12. — *Order* 5.

An oriental flower, of a rich purple color. The plant itself is very green and beautiful.

A Serenade.

Look out upon the stars, my love,
   And shame them with thine eyes,
On which, than all the lights above,
   There hang more destinies.
Night's beauty is the harmony
   Of blending shades and light;
Then, lady, up! look out and be
   A sister to the night!

Sleep not!—thine image wakes for aye
   Within my watching breast:
Sleep not!—from her soft sleep should fly,
   Who robs all hearts of rest.
Nay, lady, from thy slumbers break,
   And make this darkness gay
With looks, whose brightness well might make
   Of darker nights a day.

E. C. PINKNEY.

ELDER.

SAMBUCUS. *Class* 5. — *Order* 3.

Flowers, white. Berries, dark purple. Whole shrub medicinal.

Compassion.

Oh, let me wipe
The tears from thy too mournful eyes, and make
Thee happy, dearest, by my own true love.
I will console thee by the earnest truth
Of a confiding heart; by kindly deeds
To those who mourn; by patient love and hope
For those who go astray from the high path
Of duty; by a gentle watch o'er thee
When thou art sick and weary; and by still
And secret chastening of my own wild heart
In the dear presence of my God. Thine eye
Smiles on me while I promise—'t is enough!

EGLANTINE.

ROSA. *Class* 12. — *Order* 13.

This is a sweet-scented shrub, with delicate pink flowers. Grows often to a great height.

Poetry.

THY spirit has a gift, a secret gift,
   Which answers only to the far, bright stars,
When through the greenwood's high and changeful rift,
   Streams down the light of Venus and of Mars;
Which answers only to the winds and streams,
The sweet wood-blossoms and the moon's pale beams.

Thou seest strange beauty in the silent things
   That others idly pass. The small, wild bird
That flutters o'er the rose his bright blue wings,
   The singing brook by careless ears unheard,
The wild flower, swinging in the lonely dell—
All bind thee with a strong and wondrous spell.

EVERLASTING.

GNAPHALIUM. *Class* 19. — *Order* 2.

This is a common wild flower. Blossoms pearly white, and unwithering.

Always remembered.

I THINK of thee when the bright sunlight shimmers
    Across the sea;
When the clear fountain in the moonbeam glimmers,
    I think of thee.

I see thee, if far up the pathway yonder
    The dust be stirred;
If faint steps o'er the little bridge to wander
    At night be heard.

I hear thee, when the tossing waves' low rumbling
    Creeps up the hill;
I go to the lone wood, and listen, trembling,
    When all is still.

GOETHE.

EVERGREEN.

Class 10. — *Order* 1.

There are several genuses of Wintergreen, but nearly all belong to the same class. Among these are the *Chirraphila*, *Pyrola* and *Gaultheria*.

Poverty and Worth.

FAIR child of Poverty! thy only dower
Is thy transcendent beauty, and the gift
Which nature throws but seldom in a vase
Of such exquisite workmanship,—a heart,
Pure as the wreath round Apennines' cold brow,
And true and gentle as the constant dove.
Thy dress is coarse and simple, and thy hands,
Though small and delicate, are sparkling not
With many costly diamonds. On thy brow
No band of woven brilliants tells the tale
Of lavish partiality. Thy hair,
In its dark flowing richness, boasteth not
Of pearl, or ornament, save one wild flower,
Plucked from the sterile borders of a rock—
Fit emblem of thy lowliness and worth.

MRS. SCOTT.

FIR.

PINUS. *Class* 21. — *Order* 16.

A genus consisting of near forty species, found in Europe, North America, Barbary, India and China.

Time.

WAIT thou for Time—the slow-unfolding flower
Chides man's impatient haste with long delay;
The harvest ripening in the autumnal sun—
The golden fruit of suffering's weighty power
Within the soul—like soft bells' silvery chime
Repeat the tones, if fame may not be won,
Or if the heart, where thou shouldst find a shrine,
   Breathe forth no blessings on thy lonely way!

Wait thou for time—it hath a sorcerer's power
To dim life's mockeries that gaily shine,
To lift the veil of seeming from the real,
Bring to thy soul a rich or fearful dower,
With golden tracery on the sands of life,
And raise the drooping heart from scenes ideal
To a high purpose in the world of strife.
   Wait thou for time!

MISS LUCY HOOPER.

FLOWERING REED.

CANNA AUGUSTIFOLIA. *Class* 1. — *Order* 1.

Found in the Southern States.

Confidence in Heaven.

OH, there is solemn peace, and strength sublime,
   And holy fortitude, and deep sweet rest
In all our thoughts and visions of that clime
   Where dwell the spirits of the loved and blest.
In every hue of gladsome beauty drest,
   They come across our hearts like gleams of light,
Fraught with a mission, at God's high behest—
   A mission to relieve our mental sight
By glimpses of a life where all is calm and bright.

FORGET-ME-NOT.

VIOLA CUCULA. *Class* 5. — *Order* 1.

A very pretty, but minute flower, growing by the brooksides. Color, sky blue.

True Love.

GIVE not to weary thought the love
    That should be solely mine;
Nor tire thee of the shrinking dove
    Thou call'st so fondly thine.
I know my words are weak and small—
    For mind like thine, unmeet;
But I have love beyond them all,
    To lavish at thy feet.

Nay, heed it not, this foolish tear
    That trembles in mine eye;
It always comes when thou art here;
    I know not how, or why.
It is not grief, or pain, or joy;
    It comes of love, may be;
Then do not thou the spell destroy—
    'T is bliss to weep for thee!

FOXGLOVE.

DIGITALIS. *Class* 14. — *Order* 2.

Flowers crimson, purple, white and yellow.

I am not ambitious for myself, but for you.

THOU callest me the glorious Sun;
   Then thou the *Moon* shalt be;
For idle all the fame I've won,
   Unless conferred on thee.

I only covet dazzling light,
   That I may see *thee* shine;
And gladly hide myself from sight,
   To leave the world all thine!

Then think not I forget thee, love,
   Though high my course may be;
Not mine the laurel wreath they've wove—
   I won it, love, for thee!

FUCHSIA.

LADIES' EAR DROP. *Class* 8. — *Order* 1.

Flowers pendulous—red, with a blue centre.

Humble Love.

I LOVE thee. Yes, as flowers love light and air,
   As night its stars, or earth the glorious sun,
As the crushed heart loves lone and earnest prayer,
   So love I thee, thou true and earnest one!
And this is life—the life that thou canst give—
'T is but one thing to love thee and to live.

Deal gently, then, and suffer me to feed
   The vestal flame I vainly sought to quell ;
It shall not wrong or pain thee; but, in need,
   Shall be thy comfort, and shall serve thee well.
Though timid as the fawn that loves the wood,
I will defy all powers to do thee good.

GENTIAN.

GENTIANA. *Class* 5. — *Order* 2.

A very beautiful autumn wild flower, of a deep blue color, with delicately fringed petals.

Virgin Pride.

ALONE and pure my life shall be,
A vestal flame from passion free;
Unwon, unwooed by human love,
My heart shall fix its hopes above.

Approach me not with tempting wiles—
My lip denies thee while it smiles;
In virgin liberty and peace,
I will live out my mortal lease.

GERANIUM — ROSE.

PELAGORIUM CAPITATUM. *Class* 16. — *Order* 7.

Leaves rose-scented. Flowers purplish pink,

Preference.

OTHERS may wear a gayer smile,
   And speak in richer tones;
But ah! my heart, my heart, the while,
   Each spell, save thine, disowns.

Dearer to me one word of thine
   Than all that others speak;
My heart I lay upon thy shrine—
   Accept it ere it break.

GERANIUM — SCARLET.

P. INQUINANS.

Leaves round, velvety. Flowers a rich scarlet.

Thou art changed.

THOU lovest me not as thou lovedst me of old,
   Ere I suffered one throb of keen anguish for thee;
The fire on the shrine of thy heart hath grown cold,
   Or if burning, it burneth no longer for me.

Thou shouldst not grow weary of one so allied
   To thy destiny, dearest, as I am to thine;
Whose love, like the ivy, long planted and tried,
   Grows greenest and best on a mouldering shrine.

GERANIUM — OAK.

P. QUERCIFOLIUM.

Flowers pale blue.

True Friendship.

THERE are some spirits fitly strung
   To echo back the tones of mine;
And those few, cherished souls among,
   I dare, dear friend, to number thine.

Angels attend thee! May their wings
   Fan every shadow from thy brow;
For only bright and loving things
   Should wait on one so good as thou.

And when my prayers are pure and strong,
   As they in my best hours can be,
Amid my loved and cherished throng,
   I'll count, and pray for—*thee!*

GERANIUM — LEMON.

P. ACERIFOLIUM.

Leaves palmate, serrate. Flowers white.

Tranquillity of Mind.

THOU art more blest, I deem,
Than in thy gayer hours, though grief hath laid
Its surgeon hand upon thy heart, and left
Some aching wounds. Oh, truly blest alone
Are they, who, by the wondrous deeds of time,
Gentle or stern, have learned the holy peace
Which dwells with God; who have been taught to seek
A deeper love from Him; a love more pure
And firm than that which dwells in human hearts,
And throws a transient glory o'er the earth.

Peace with thee
Makes its abiding home; and though the world,
With its consuming pleasures, comes not here,
Yet Faith, and Hope, and Charity are thine,
With all their sweets. Such peace as theirs, this world
Can neither give, nor can it take away.

GERANIUM — SILVER-LEAVED.

P. ARGENTIFOLIUM.

This has a beautiful silvery leaf.

Recall.

COME back, oh come! The past shall be
    A cloud fore'er removed;
Come back, and in my welcome see
    How thou art still beloved.

I strove in vain to bid my heart
    Forget its early dream;
For ah! the dream would not depart,
    And thou wert still its theme.

Come back, and never more shall doubt
    Or cold distrust be mine;
My heart hath cast those demons out,
    And now is wholly thine.

GILLY FLOWER.

CHEIRANTHUS. *Class* 15. — *Order* 2.

Flowers bright red, purple or white. The white gilly flower is very fragrant.

Lasting Beauty.

Oh faint, indeed, are outward hues
  Compared with thy rich mental light;
Each day thy thoughts their rays diffuse,
  Yet grow each added day more bright.

To scatter charms so rich as thine,
  In vain time's surging billows roll;
The pearls that on thy forehead shine,
  Are gathered, daily, from thy soul.

GOLDEN ROD.

SOLIDAGO. *Class* 19. — *Order* 2.

A North American genus. Flowers bright yellow, and very showy.

Encouragement.

I WILL not chide thy love,
    Nor crush its budding flower;
But it must look above,
    For fostering sun and shower.

May be, when months are o'er,
    This heart may be all thine;
Oh, wouldst thou ask for more
    From lips reserved as mine?

GRAPE.

VITIS. *Class* 5. — *Order* 1.

Flowers numerous, light green. There are many species of wild grape in North America-some very fine.

Charity.

SPEAK kindly, oh speak soothingly
  To him whose hopes are crossed,
Whose blessed trust in human love
  Was early, early lost;
For wearily—how wearily!
  Drags life, if love depart;
Oh, let the balm of gentle words
  Fall on the smitten heart!

Go gladly, with true sympathy,
  Where want's pale victims pine,
And bid life's sweetest smiles again
  Along their pathway shine.
Oh, heavily doth poverty
  Man's nobler instincts bind;
Yet sever not that chain to cast
  A *sadder* on the mind.

MRS. CASE.

GRASS.

GRAMINA. *Class* 3. — *Order* 2.

There are more than three hundred species of Grass. Some have very pretty flowers.

Submission.

I AM resigned. Whate'er my fate may be,—
 Or storms or sunshine, to *Thy* will I bow;
And be the fruit that hangs on life's green tree
 Or sweet or bitter, it is welcome now.
All things are equal to the heart that bears
A faith unblenching through earth's thousand snares.

I am resigned. In holy hope and trust,
 I wait the coming of a brighter day;
And though but thorns, and rocks, and scorching dust
 Lie all along my melancholy way,
Yet with a fervent heart and willing mind,
I can look up and say, *I am resigned!*

HAWTHORN.

CRATEGUS. *Class* 12. — *Order* 5.

Principally a North American genus. Flowers white. Berries scarlet.

Hope.

HOPE on, hope ever!
Dark o'er us now the clouds of grief are brooding,
  Hoarsely the streamlets murmur at our feet;
Bright birds of song, our eager grasp eluding,
  Far from our tree of love and life retreat.
But oh! not yet, my gentle friend, shall leave us
  The fervent hope of sunshine and of joy;
And whatsoe'er of wrong may come to grieve us,
  Let there be one thing grief can ne'er destroy—
    Hope on, hope ever!

HAZEL.

CORYLUS. *Class* 20. — *Order* 13.

This shrub is well known to children for its sweet palatable nut. The shrub, itself, is green and pretty.

Reconciliation.

We have been friends together—it cannot all be o'er!
Oh, let us nurse the smothered spark, till it shall blaze once more!
Here, take this hand; as once you deemed, its grasp is warm and true,
And in my heart a gushing fount of love still springs for you.
Oh, bless that beaming smile! it comes all sorrow to dispel;
We're friends once more together—I will not say farewell!

MRS. SAWYER.

HELIOTROPE.

HELIOTROPIUM. *Class* 5. — *Order* 1.

Flowers white or faint purple. Very sweet scented. Turns toward the sun.

Devotion.

AH, I would sit for long, long hours
    And let thee read my heart—
Its Greek, and poetry, and flowers,
    And words of cunning art,
And never think, with all thy skill,
    That thou couldst make it plain,
For something thou wouldst find there still
    To study o'er again.

Deep graved upon its secret leaves
    Are mysteries so rare,
That all the aid thy mind receives
    From books, would fail thee there.
But I, yes I, with simple pride,
    Could soon explain the key;
Here, take this sentence for thy guide—
    My love for GOD *and* THEE!

HIBISCUS.

HIBISCUS. *Class* 16. — *Order* 13.

A kind of Mallows. Flowers white and purple, or a faint straw-color and purple.

Beauty is vain.

SEEK for beauty if thou wilt,
But mark the quality; not that which shines
From human face divine, and gains applause
From gaping starers—that which fools admire,
And seek no other—but that higher kind
Which earth not only approbates, but heaven;
Pure, bright, celestial! Beauty of the soul—
BEAUTY OF HOLINESS!

J. G. ADAMS.

HOLLYHOCK.

ALCEA. *Class* 16. — *Order* 13.

A native of the East. Flowers of a variety of colors—single and double.

Ambition.

My laurel-wreath with blood is stained—
 How great hath been its cost!
What is the glory I have gained,
 Compared with what I've lost?—
Earth's proudest ones have sought my shrine,
 And offered incense there—
But gladly would I all resign,
 A *quiet heart* to bear!

C. A. FILLEBROWN.

Ah! peace is never found in pleasure's whirl,
Nor where Ambition's luring meteors burn.
'These bring no lasting joy; in *humble worth*
Lies all the enduring glory of this earth.

S. C. E.

HONEYSUCKLE.

LONICERA. *Class* 5. — *Order* 1.

Flowers white, red, scarlet, and yellow. Very fragrant and beautiful.

Fidelity.

I GO with thee! I will be thine
   In weal, in want, in wo;
Thy path, where'er it leads, is mine—
   I go, my love, I go!

'T is not for wealth I seek the shade
   Of forest bower and tree;
To share the burdens on thee laid—
   For *this* I go with thee!

HOP.

HUMULUS. *Class* 21. — *Order* 5.

Flowers yellow-green. Grows very luxuriantly.

Injustice.

OH, it was not the sordid fear
   Planted in common minds that shook
His upright frame, and drew the tear
   From his seared brain! 't was not the look
Of ghastly death—ah, no! ah, no!
   'T was *wounded feeling*, crushed and flung
All poisoned back, like drops that flow
   The fatal Upas-tree among!

MRS. SCOTT.

HOUSTONIA.

HOUSTONIA CERULEA. *Class* 4. — *Order* 1.
Venus' Pride.

A small, delicate spring-flower. White or pale blue.

Quiet Happiness.

COME to our cottage, love. How sweetly there
The rose-trees bloom! How the soft scented air
Plays round its shaded trellises, and floats
Through our own quiet rooms The woodlark's notes,
The sweetest in the choir of earth, awake
Our happy spirits to the day, and make
Our morning hymn of praise. The mellow beams
Of the rich sun shine gently on the streams
That murmur there; and thy pure, faithful love
Smiles on me ever!

HYDRANGEA.

HYDRANGEA. *Class* 10. — *Order* 2.

Flowers rose-color, sometimes blue. Hue very changeable.

Heartlessness.

YES, thou canst smile and be as gay.
  As though no heart thy guile had broken;
While every step along *my* way
  Brings up of thee some painful token.

Thou breathest in a dozen ears
  The same fond words once breathed to me;
While I, alas! in secret tears,
  Can only think and dream of thee.

ICE-PLANT.

MESEMBRYANTHEMUM. *Class* 12. — *Order* 5.

Resembles the Dew-plant very much, but has a frostier appearance. Flowers of a pale rose-color.

Your looks freeze me.

Oh, turn away those rigid eyes!
My heart hath frozen 'neath their spell;
Such looks are not the meet replies
To one who loveth thee so well.

One smile—ah, one frank, tender smile
Were than a thousand gems more dear,
If it but told my heart the while,
That I had power thy thoughts to cheer.

IRIS.

IRIS. *Class* 3. — *Order* 1. Fleur-de-lis.

Flowers of various colors—commonly blue.

A Message.

WERE not thy spirit purified to look
Through all things beautiful to God and heaven,
These gentle readings from love's holy book
    Had not been given.

Were thine eye sealed to those sweet lessons, taught
In the dim oracles of leaf and tree,
I had not made them messengers of thought,
    Dear friend, to thee.

But take them now, for they will talk to thee
In the sweet accents of poetic lore;
Heed their soft pleadings—kindly *'think of me'*—
    I ask no more.

IVY.

HEDERA. *Class* 5. — *Order* 1.

Flowers green. Berries round and black.

I have found one true heart.

LONG have I sought, and vainly have I yearned
To meet some spirit that could answer mine;
Then chide me not that I so soon have learned
    To talk with thine.

Oh, thou wilt cherish what some hearts would spurn,
So gentle and so full of soul thou art;
And shrine my feelings in that holy urn—
    Thine own true heart.

JASMINE.

JASMIMUM. *Class* 2. — *Order* 1.

An Asiatic genus. Flowers, white and very sweet. Plant climbing.

Amiability.

THINE is that excelling virtue
　The pure-hearted only know;
Thine that unassuming goodness
　Which in silent deeds doth flow.
Thou dost make the poor and needy
　In thy presence to rejoice;
All the bowed and broken-hearted
　Love thy peace-inspiring voice.

MRS. SCOTT.

JONQUIL.

NARCISSUS. *Class* 16. — *Order* 1.

Flowers golden, emitting a pleasant but powerful perfume.

Affection returned.

THAT thou art loved, this flower my witness be!
   In the bright morning, noon, or starry night,
One thought my bosom fills—it is of *thee!*
   And thou dost make all hours and seasons bright.

To see thee, hear thee, know that thou art nigh,
   Oh, this is joy unknown to me before!
All other thoughts are gone when thou art by—
   Thou fill'st my heart—it can contain no more!

KING CUP.

RANUNCULUS. *Class* 3. — *Order* 13. Butter Cup.

A very glossy, yellow flower, common in our fields in June. It is sometimes found double, in gardens.

I wish I was rich.

Oh, had I wealth, upon thy shrine
   I'd pour its lavish treasures forth,
And every jewel should be thine
   That glistens in the sea or earth.

Oh, had I wealth, no want should come
   To breathe its blight upon thy heart;
And round thy rich and beauteous home
   Should cluster every gem of art.

Oh, had I wealth, I'd lay it all
   With pride and pleasure at thy feet;
And thou shouldst shine in home and hall,
   The fairest that the eye could meet.

LABURNUM.

CYTISUS. *Class* 17. — *Order* 4.

Flowers purplish, or yellow.

Pensive Beauty.

THOUGHT, like a bird of drooping wing,
    Sits hushed upon thy brow;
While from thine eyes' deep, shaded spring,
    A thousand feelings flow.

Thou art like some lone, brilliant star,
    Some planetary light,
That glitters, radiant and afar,
    Within the depths of night.

Thy beauty has a twilight grace,
    Half-shadowy and half-bright—
A curtain o'er thy radiant face
    Of intellectual light.

LADY'S SLIPPER.

CYPRIPEDIUM. *Class* 20. — *Order* 2.

A small genus, of which six species are found in North America. Flowers purple, pink, yellow, etc.

Capricious Beauty.

CHANGING ever, who can dare
Trust his feelings to thy care?
Smiling now, and now so vexed,
Who knows what to look for next?
Who can love thee if they would;
Or *would* love thee if they could?
What but agony and fear,
First a smile and then a tear,
Could attend a true devotion
To a heart of such commotion?
Nay, capricious one! believe me,
Thine no more the power to grieve me!

LARKSPUR.

DELPHINIUM. *Class* 13. — *Order* 3.

Flowers blue, white and pink. A very handsome, showy blossom, easy of cultivation.

Inconstancy.

THOU art not what thou wert,
   Farewell, and may God bless thee!
My heart with strength is girt
   Once more to say, God bless thee!

Thou hast forgot thy vow—
   I give thee back its token;
'T is but a memory now
   Of pledges lightly broken.

Farewell! we meet no more;
   And though I now regret thee,
My grief will soon be o'er;
   I can, and *will*, forget thee!

LAUREL.

KALMIA. *Class* 10. — *Order* 1.

A magnificent American shrub. Foliage a deep, glossy green; flowers beautiful, mostly white, though often of a delicate carmine, or rose-pink color.

Virtue is true Beauty.

OH, not in the *outward world* alone,
May THE BEAUTIFUL be to the soul made known;
In its own far depths, *in its inner life*,
Silent and pure is its spirit rife.
Seen in the *Love* that is still the same
In the captive's dungeon, the martyr's flame,
As it is in the hour of joy and light,
When life is unclouded, and hope is bright.
Seen in the *Mercy*, gentle and nigh
To the destitute's moan, the sufferer's sigh;
In the tear of *Repentance*; the widow's *mite*;
The *Truth* that is firm to the good and right;
In *Meekness, Forgiveness, Humility, Prayer,*
In *Hope* that can suffer, and *Faith* that can bear,
In deeds and in motives untold by the tongue,
By chisel uncarved, by poet unsung,—
THE BEAUTIFUL *lives in the depths of the soul!*

E. H. CHAPIN.

LAVENDER.

LAVENDULA. *Class* 14. — *Order* 1.

Flowers blue, and white. Delightfully aromatic.

Acknowledgment.

AH! must I tell thee? Well, I fear
   The die is surely cast;
That I am thine, and only thine,
   Beloved, to the last!

I could not see thee, hear thy voice,
   Or look upon thy brow,
Nor fail to love thee tenderly—
   My heart must break or bow!

LEMON.

CITRUS. *Class* 13. — *Order* 1.

A native of warm climates. Flowers small, white.

Discretion.

'T is better, far, than beauty, or the grace
That captivates the eye, that sober charm
Of thine, which o'er thy words and deeds
Keeps constant vigilance. A steward, thou,
Faithful to the best riches of thy soul;
And he who puts his trust in one like thee,
'Mid all his cares will find unbroken rest.

LETTUCE.

LACTUTA. *Class* 18. — *Order* 1.

A common garden vegetable. Flowers yellow.

Cold-hearted.

WHAT matters all the nobleness
  Which in her breast resideth,
And what the warmth and tenderness
  Her mien of coldness hideth,
If but ungenerous thoughts prevail
When thou her bosom wouldst assail,
While tenderness and warmth doth ne'er,
By any chance, toward thee appear?

C. F. HOFFMAN.

LILAC.

SYRINGA. *Class* 2. — *Order* 1.

Too well known to need description. Flowers purple, and white.

First Emotion of Love.

How sweet and rapturous 't is to feel
Ourselves exalted in a lovely soul,—
To know our joys make glow another's cheek,
Our fears do tremble in another's heart,
Our sufferings bedew another's eye!

SCHILLER.

As the little floweret hideth
By the woodland stream,
So in youthful hearts abideth
Love's first witching dream.

MISS J. A. FLETCHER.

LILY — WHITE.

LILIUM CANDIDUM. *Class* 6. — *Order* 1.

A native of Palestine. Very fragrant.

Purity.

Ask me not why I should love her:
    Look upon those soul-full eyes!
Look while mirth or feeling move her,
    And see there how sweetly rise
Thoughts gay and gentle from a breast,
Which is of innocence the nest—
Which, though each joy were from it fled,
By truth would still be tenanted!

                  C. F. HOFFMAN.

LILY OF THE VALLEY.

CONVALLARIA. *Class* 6. — *Order* 1.

Flowers small and white, with greenish veins. Pendulous.

The heart withering in secret.

AH, fare thee well, thou loved and worshipped one!
  For death is at my heart; such death as steals
To the young leaf, when autumn frost and sun
  Tinge all its veins with beauty which conceals
'Neath radiant dyes the wasting of its heart.—
So shall I, too, in quiet smiles depart.

LOCUST.

ROBINA. *Class* 17. — *Order* 10.

A very handsome ornamental tree or shrub. Blossoms white and fragrant.

Affection beyond the grave.

WHAT though the loving heart is wrung
By chilling words of cold farewell?
And o'er its dying hopes is flung
    Their echoing knell?

Shall we not meet in that bright land
Where parting words are never spoken?
And love is not a brittle band
    So lightly broken?

Shall we not all meet there to love,
With love that has no trembling fears?
In that dear home, far, far above
    This land of tears?

LUPINE.

LUPINUS. *Class* 17. — *Order* 4.

Flowers white, blue, yellow and rose-colored. The common wild Lupine is of a purplish-blue color.

Dejection, Sorrow.

I WOULD not stay forever here
   In this sad world of care and pain;
I would not have life linger on,
   Or give my thoughts to earth again.
I long to close my tearful eyes,
   Recline my weary, aching head
Upon the couch where all is peace,
   And rest among the early dead.

*

Inwove with many a darkening thread
   The texture of my life appears;
How vain were all its sweetest hopes,
   How more than bitter were its tears!

MISS M. A. DODD.

LONDON PRIDE.

SILENE. *Class* 10. — *Order* 3.

A tall, scarlet flower. Resembles the Catchfly, of which it is a species.

Frivolity.

LIFE should have higher, nobler aims
    Than mirth, and song, and dance;
Oh then from sport and idle games,
    To higher deeds advance.
Throw by thy foolish wit and songs,
    Thy graceful tricks of art,
And far from fashion's heartless throngs
    Add wisdom to thy heart.

MALLOWS.

LAVATERA. *Class* 16. — *Order* 13.

This is a very delicate, but scentless garden flower. Flowers white or bright pink.

Sweet Disposition.

THE friend we love is youthful and fair,
And gentle and pure as the angels are;
Sincerity dwells in her earnest eyes,
And her soul is warm as the Southern skies!
Oh, the friend we love is a friend indeed,
She's ever true in the hour of need!

MRS. SCOTT.

MAPLE.

ACER. *Class* 8. — *Order* 1.

Eton mentions eight species of the maple, five of which are large trees, and valuable both for timber and saccharine matter.

Reserve.

>A VEIL is round thee,—and thy heart
>   Is like a hidden flower;
> But could we see thee as thou art,
>   We should confess thy power.
>
> Oh, throw that modest screen aside,
>   And let us read thy heart;
> Thou canst not *all* its goodness hide—
>   Oh why, then, veil a part?

MARIGOLD.

CALENDULA. *Class* 19. — *Order* 4.

A brilliant yellow flower—very common.

Contempt.

LEAVE me to my lot!
Be it or death or slavery, it were bliss
To what thy love would proffer! *I am free!*
Talk to the wild bird battling with the storm,
Of shelter in the cage; or woo the kid
From the bluff rocks to nestle at thy feet;
But mock not *me* with bribes!

MIGNONETTE.

RESEDA ODORATA. *Class* 11. — *Order* 3.

Flowers very fragrant. Color white, with yellow stamens.

Moral and Intellectual Beauty.

BEAUTY consists not in the sparkling eye,
The damask cheek and lip, or forehead high;
Not in the graceful form, or glistening hair,
Or melody of voice! Oh no! not there.
But in the SOUL which every glance displays
Basking forever in affection's rays,—
Speaking in love's soft tones, with sunlight smile,
Which can an aching heart from wo beguile!
It dwelleth there in majesty supreme,
Sweeter than music's voice, or seraph's dream!

MISS H. J. WOODMAN.

MIMOSA.

MIMOSA. *Class* 16. — *Order* 10.

Flowers pale purple, contracting when touched.

Sensitiveness.

YOUR heart is a music box, dearest!
  With exquisite tunes at command,
Of melody sweetest and clearest,
  If tried by a delicate hand;
But its workmanship, love, is so fine,
  At a single rude touch it would break:
Then oh! be the magic key mine,
  Its fairy-like whispers to wake!

MRS. F. S. OSGOOD.

MOSS.

SYCOPODIUM. *Class* 22. — *Order* 2.

Mosses are too obscure and irregular for ordinary distinction; yet are greatly admired for their verdure and beauty.

Maternal Love.

NUMBER thy lamps of love, and tell me now
How many canst thou re-light at the stars,
And blush not at their burning? One—one only—
Lit while your pulses by one heart kept time,
And fed with faithful fondness to your grave—
(Though sometimes with a hand stretched back from heaven)
Steadfast through all things—near when most forgot—
And with its finger of unerring truth
Pointing the lost way in thy darkest hour—
One lamp—*thy Mother's love*—amid the stars
Shall lift its pure flame changeless, and before
The throne of God burn through eternity—
Holy—as it was lit and lent thee here.

N. P. WILLIS.

MYRTLE.

MYRTUS. *Class* 12. — *Order* 1.

A beautiful tree, held in high estimation by the ancients. Flowers white.

Love in Absence.

I MISS thee each lone hour,
  Star of my heart!
No other voice hath power
  Joy to impart.
I listen for thy hasty step,
  Thy kind, sweet tone;
But sorrowing silence whispers me,
  Thou art alone!

Darkness is on the hearth—
  Nought do I say;
Books are but little worth—
  Thou art away!
Voices, the true and kind,
  Strange are to me;
I have lost heart and mind,
  Thinking of thee.

MRS. SCOTT.

NASTURTION.

TROPEOLUM. *Class* 8. — *Order* 1.

Flowers golden yellow. Very brilliant. Plant somewhat creeping.

Patriotism.

HAIL to the land whereon we tread,
 Our fondest boast!

*

There is no other land like thee,
 No dearer shore;
Thou art the shelter of the free,
The home, the port of liberty,
Thou hast been, and shalt ever be,
 Till time is o'er.
Ere I forget to think upon
My land, shall mother curse the son
 She bore.

J. G. PERCIVAL

NIGHTSHADE.

SOLANUM. *Class* 5. — *Order* 1.

More than one hundred species of this plant are found in America. Flowers yellow, blue, white and purple.

Dark Thoughts.

MARCH—march—march!
   Earth groans as they tread!
Each carries a skull,
   Going down to the dead!
Every stride, every stamp,
   Every footfall is bolder;
'T is a skeleton's tramp,
   With a skull on his shoulder!
But ho! how he steps
   With a high-tossing head,
That clay-covered bone,
   Going down to the dead!

A. C. COXE.

OAK.

QUERCUS. *Class* 21. — *Order* 13.

The Oak embraces about eighty species. Only one is found in the Southern hemisphere.

Hospitality.

THANKS for the kindly courtesies
   Beside thy hearthstone shared;
Be every joy that round it lies,
   And every blessing spared!

The roof that over me hath spread
   A shelter kind and warm,
Oh, may it shield thy generous head
   From every chilling storm!

For kind, indeed, have been thy cares
   Since 'neath its shade I came;
I've shared in all *thy* household prayers—
   Thou shalt in *mine* the same.

OLEANDER.

NERIUM. *Class* 5. — *Order* 2.

A beautiful flowered exotic. It grows to the size of a small tree.

Beware!

I KNOW they have pleaded, the friends that are round thee;
    I know they have warned thee, entreated and wept ;
They have shown thee the guile in the spell that hath bound thee,
    And the serpent whose coils round thy spirit have crept.
Yet still the grim cavern yawns wide to receive thee,
    And now while no terrors thy spirit oppress,
I urge this last prayer, not to frighten or grieve thee,
    Oh, no! but to save thee, redeem thee, and bless.
I pray thee, beseech thee, if e'er thou hast loved me,
    By all our past sorrows, and trials, and tears,
By all the caprices with which thou hast proved me,
    Return to the truth of thine earlier years!

ORANGE FLOWERS.

CITRUS. *Class* 12. — *Order* 12.

Native of Asia. Flowers white and odoriferous.

Woman's Worth.

THIS, oh this, is woman's lot—
   To be a friend when others fail;
To look on death and fear it not;
   To smile when other cheeks grow pale;

To trust 'mid danger and 'mid care;
   To love when love seems almost dead;
To hope when other hearts despair;
   And pray when love and hope are fled.

MRS. MUNROE.

PANSY.

VIOLA TRICOLOR. *Class* 5. — *Order* 1.

This flower has three colors—purple, yellow and blue. It is much cultivated, and highly esteemed.

Tender and pleasant thoughts.

I HAVE Sweet thoughts of thee!
They come around me like the voice of song;
They come like birds that to the South belong,
And wear a gayer wing, and brighter crest,
Than those that on the rooftree build the nest;
They come more tender, beautiful, and bright,
Than any thoughts that *others* can excite;
They tell me gentle tales of thee and thine,
Of gems of truth that in thy spirit shine,
Of goodness, purity, and holy zeal,
That can for others earnest pity feel;
Of all things beautiful in soul and heart,—
And *such* they tell me, dearest, that thou art!

PASSION FLOWER.

PASSIFLORA. *Class* 16. — *Order* 2.

Indigenous to America. At the South, the flowers are bright red. Those of the North are generally pale blue or yellow.

Religious Fervor.

How should the soul with adoration glow,
   To that great Power, eternal and supreme,
Who gives us faculties for joy and wo,
   And hope and reason guarding each extreme;
Who paints on sorrow's clouds the rainbow-beam
   That cheers our spirits through sad mists of tears,
And bids the heaven-lit taper brighter gleam,
   As down the dark declivity of years
We seek the better clime, where Truth her temple rears!

MRS. BROUGHTON.

PEA — EVERLASTING.

LATHYRUS LATIFOLIA. *Class* 17. — *Order* 4.

Flowers, of the native kind, purple; the exotic, crimson.

Wilt thou go?

ONE moment o'er my chequered path
　Thy smile hath shed its gladdening ray;
A rainbow on a cloud of wrath—
　And wilt thou, also, go away?

*

Thou 'rt going! Well, thou knowest
　What prayers arise for thee;
And wheresoe'er thou goest,
　Bear gentle thoughts of me.

PEA — SWEET.

LATHYRUS ODORATUS. *Class* 17. — *Order* 4.

Very beautiful, and possessing much of the fragrance of the pink. The flowers are variegated with blue, lilac, rose, white, etc.

Departure.

UNNOTICED fell the sere and yellow leaf,
   Unheeded swept the moaning breezes by;
The fading flowers awoke no throb of grief,
   There was no sadness in the wind's low sigh;
Could gloom or sorrow cloud the dying year,
When *thou*, the summer of my heart, wert here?

One hour hath passed—and o'er the deep blue sky
   A dimness hangs, whose chill is in my heart;
The wind with funeral moans goes sweeping by,
   And asks in every whisper where thou art;
The sunshine hath gone with thee and the flowers,
And frost hath chained the fairy-footed hours.

PEACH BLOSSOM.

AMYGDALUS. *Class* 12. — *Order* 1.

Flowers beautiful rose or pink color.

I am your captive.

OH, is it sin to love the very air
   That once hath rested on thy beaming brow?
To gaze in fondness on thy vacant chair,
   And on thy books and flowers deserted now?
Or turn in worship on that pictured face,
Whose sweetest looks the heart alone can trace?

Is it a sin to live again each hour
   Passed in thy presence? To recall thy tones,
Thy playful words, thy serious thoughts, whose power
   Thrills every nerve my quickened spirit owns?
Is it a crime to worship and adore
What is so good the Ideal asks no more?

PETUNIA.

PETUNIA. *Class* 5. — *Order* 1.

A beautiful procumbent plant, blossoming through the season. Corolla funnel-form; color white or purple; the latter sometimes edged with green. The white species is very fragrant.

Thou art less proud than they deem thee.

> They say that thou art proud; *I* know
>   Meek thoughts oft o'er thee stealing;
> I know the silent, generous flow
>   Of fervent, kindly feeling
> Thy heart yields—by these and many a token
> I know thou 'rt less proud than thine *eye* hath spoken.

ROSE OF SHARON, 1844.

PEONY.

PÆONIA. Class 13. — *Order* 3.

Superb double flowers. Colors crimson and white. Root perennial.

Ostentation.

I GRIEVE to see thee vain and proud—I grieve
That this world's honors have enticed thy heart,
Such haughty airs become thee not. For me,
I better love a modest mien and look
Than all the gaudy tinsel wealth can buy,
Or vanity display. Put by thy pride,
And by a holy life earn nobler praise
Than such as pomp and idle show can win.

PHLOX.

PHLOX. *Class* 5. — *Order* 1.

Flowers purple, pink, lilac and white. Root perennial. A native of North America.

Our souls are united.

WHERE'ER thou goest, I will go;
   Where'er thou diest, die;
Together in one humble grave
   Our senseless dust shall lie.

And I will love thy chosen friends—
   Thy people shall be mine;
And we will kneel to praise one God
   Before one common shrine.

Our souls—ah, what shall part our souls?
   In ties of love entwined,
They will defy the spells and chains
   That even death can bind.

PINE.

PINUS. *Class* 21. — *Order* 16.

Found from Canada to Carolina. Leaves dark green and glossy.

Time and Faith.

WAIT thou for Time, but to thy heart take Faith,
Soft beacon-light upon a stormy sea:
A mantle for the pure in heart, to pass
Through a dim world, untouched by living death,
  A cheerful watcher through the spirit's night,
Soothing the grief from which she may not flee—
  A herald of glad news—a scraph bright,
Pointing to sheltering havens yet to be.

MISS LUCY HOOPER.

PINK — WHITE.

DIANTHUS ALBUS. *Class* 10. — *Order* 2.

Root perennial. Flowers very fragrant.

Lovely and pure Affection.

I NEVER have loved thee—yet strange tho' it be,
So soft are the feelings I cherish for thee,
That the wildest of passions could never impart
More joy to my soul, or more bliss to my heart.
They come o'er my breast in my happiest hours,
They come like the south wind that ruffles the flowers,
A thrilling of softness, a thrilling of bliss—
Say, is there no name for a passion like this?

It cannot be friendship—it cannot be love;
Yet I know the sweet feeling descends from above,
For it takes from my bosom no portion of ease,
Yet adds all the rapture, the pleasure of these;
For so soft the emotion my spirit hath nursed,
It is warm as the last, and more pure than the first;
For my heart when near thine grows soft as a dove—
Yet it cannot be friendship—it cannot be love.

MRS. AMELIA B. WELBY.

PINK — RED.

DIANTHUS RUBEUS. *Class* 10. — *Order* 2.

The Dianthus has many beautiful varieties. The double red pink is one of its most beautiful.

Woman's Love.

MAN's love lives but with hope; while woman's heart
Still echoes to the music of the past.

*

A love all sacrifice and suffering; a star
That gathers lustre from the gloom of night;
A martyr's fond idolatry; a faith
Baptized in tears, to sorrow consecrate.

MRS. WHITMAN.

POLYANTHUS.

PRIMULA AURICULA. *Class* 5. — *Order* 1.

A native of the Alps. Originally yellow, but by cultivation assumes various colors. Perennial.

Confidence.

'Trust in thee!' Ay, dearest, there's no one but must,
Unless truth be a fable, in such as thee trust!
For who can see heaven's own hue in those eyes,
And doubt that truth with it came down from the skies;
While each thought of thy bosom, like morning's young light,
Almost ere 't is born, flashes there on his sight!

C. F. HOFFMAN.

POTATO.

SOLANUM. *Class* 5. — *Order* 1.

Flowers white or purple, with yellow anthers.

Beneficence.

In deeds of charity thy soul delights;
In mercy, justice, and in human rights;
Thy liberal heart deviseth liberal things;
Thy hand o'er every path some sunbeam flings;
The poor look up with blessings on thy face,
The children rush to meet thy kind embrace,
The weak appeal to thee for just redress,
The sorrowing throng thy path to praise and bless,
And all, of every station, age and race,
Implore thy favor, and extol thy grace.

POPPY.

PAPAVER. *Class* 13. — *Order* 1.

Of this plant *opium* is made. Flowers scarlet, purple, crimson and white.

Forgetfulness.

LET the deep waters of oblivion roll.
O'er all that irritates or grieves thy soul;
Let Time its drapery of ivy throw
O'er every painful monument of wo;
And in forgetfulness thy sorrows lose,
Since this is all the refuge thou canst choose,
Wherein to hide thy heart from Memory's pangs,
Or flee the cloud that o'er thy pathway hangs.

PRIMROSE.

PRIMULA. *Class* 5. — *Order* 1.

One of the earliest of our Spring flowers, and frequently passes under the name of Polyanthus, from which it widely differs. Flowers purple and yellow.

Modest Worth.

THINE excellence is of a rare degree;
Though praised by others 't is unknown to thee;
In humble deeds of love, and kindly care
To those who in earth's riches own no share;
By acts of mercy all unseen of men,
By silent victory over pride and sin,
By faith, and hope, and charity on earth,
Thou provest to others thy transcendent worth;
Whilst to thyself thy goodness is unknown—
Though virtue crowns and claims thee for her own.

PRIMROSE — EVENING.

ŒNOTHERA ODORATA. *Class* 8. — *Order* 1.

This plant is two or three feet high. Flowers pale yellow, and open suddenly.

I am more faithful than thou.

HAST forgotten the days, love, the long-vanished days,
   When our spirits communed through the bird and the flower;
When the stars linked our thoughts by their glittering rays,
   In a chain that had more than electrical power?

Those days were the violet blossoms of love—
   Young flowers that have faded and shrunk from thy view;
But though withered, forgotten, to thee they may prove,
   They are pressed to *one* heart ever faithful and true.

ROSE-BUD.

ROSA. *Class* 12. — *Order* 13.

The *moss* rose-bud is distinguished for its beauty.

Confession of Love.

I DO believe that unto thee
Truth, honor, plain sincerity,
  Are jewels far before
All that the others think are dear;
And yet far more than they I fear,
Because I love thee more.

And yet I hope, because I love
With thoughts that set thee far above
  Vain Fortune's glittering store;
Others may deem thou canst be won
By things that sparkle in the sun,
  But oh! I love thee more!

G. P. R. JAMES.

ROSE — BRIDAL.

RUBUS ROSAFOLIUS. *Class* 12. — *Order* 13.

This belongs to the *Bramble* family. The flowers are small, white, double, and very beautiful.

Happy Love.

It has been said that love doth bind the heart
    More strongly to the fading things of earth;
Not so with us; our spirits have no part
    With feelings which are but of mortal birth;
We love for heaven—let heaven become our home,
Ere yet the angel beckon us to come!

And are you happy? asks some gentle one
    In low, soft accents and with thoughtful eye;
Yes, dear, and more than happy, though the sun
    Is softly clouded, and the deep, blue sky
Grows deeper that it is not flushed with light,
Though all the clouds that shade it are of white.

ROSE — BURGUNDY.

ROSA PARVIFOLIA.

Leaflet fine. Flowers small.

Simplicity and Beauty.

THY beauty wins my heart
   By its unstudied grace;
There is no show of art
   In thy sweet, radiant face;
But soft simplicity and youth,
And gentle love and sunny truth
Around thy face a spell have thrown,
That wins and makes me all thine own!

ROSE — DAMASK.

ROSA DAMASCENA.

Flowers white and red. Brought from Damascus.

Bashful Love.

The blushing rose that hangs its head,
Or meets the sun with shrinking dread,
Conceals within its heart a flame
Which from that glowing noontide came.

So have *I* loved;—but some strange spell
Forbids my heart its tale to tell;
Here,—take this simple rose, and *feel*
The love my lips dare not reveal.

ROSE — MOSS.

ROSA MUSCOSA.

Flowers bright crimson—very fragrant. Sometimes the blossoms are white or pink.

Superior Merit.

I NEVER saw a form before
  Of such unrivalled loveliness,
Nor one who was of earth, who wore
  The look of heaven upon her face.
I never knew a heart so kind,
  Such tears for others' misery flow,
Nor saw a hand so gladly bind
  The crushed and bleeding heart of wo.

Her spirit was from sin so free,
  Such gladness round her path she shed,
That all, who knew her purity,
  Poured blessings on her bright young head.
In this cold world I never found
  But one to whom my heart was dear,
But thousand chords of love had bound
  Her being to this changeful sphere.

MISS PHŒBE CAREY.

ROSE — MULTIFLORA.

ROSA MULTIFLORA.

A shrub of luxuriant growth. Flowers pink, in clusters.

Grace.

THY looks how lovely! and thy face
So eloquent with mental grace!
Thy motions are as light and free
As zephyrs o'er a summer sea!
Thou art, in truth, a wayward child,
Thy words so gay, thy steps so wild;
And none can see thee speak or move
Without some glow akin to love!

ROSE — WHITE.

ROSA ALBA.

One of the most fragrant of the whole genus *Rosa*.

Too young to love.

THOU art looking now at the birds, Genie,
   But oh, do not wish their wing;
That would tempt the fowler, Genie,—
   Stay thou on earth and sing.
Stay in the nursing nest, Genie,
   Be not soon thence beguiled;
Thou wilt ne'er find a second, Genie,
   Never be twice a child.

                MISS JEWSBURY.

ROSE — RED-LEAVED.

ROSA RUBRIFOLIA.

The whole plant is more or less tinged with red.

Diffidence.

How many things I would confess,
But for this foolish bashfulness!
How often on my lip hath hung
The tale from eager passion wrung,
While foolish diffidence and fear
Have chilled my lip and kept me here!
How oft I've yearned to seek thy side,
And tell thee all with joy and pride;
But when I sought thy loved retreat,
Distrust and doubt still chained my feet!

SAGE.

SALVIA. *Class* 2. — *Order* 1.

Medicinal. Flowers blue.

Domestic Virtues.

How happy he, who to his hearth
Can woo domestic love and worth!
How sweet are fireside joys! How dear
The charms that please and soothe us here!
'The gentle tone, the ready hand,
The smile so winning and so bland,
The noiseless step, the household grace,
The soft and bright, but thoughtful face,
The fireside virtues grave and still,
Neatness, and industry, and skill,—
Oh, do not these exceed in worth
The costliest jewels of the earth?
And do they not deserve man's pride
More than all earthly wealth beside?

SNAPDRAGON.

ANTIRRHINUM. *Class* 14. — *Order* 2.

The garden Snapdragon is a procumbent plant, with purple and yellow flowers.

You are dazzling, but dangerous.

I LOVE thee not. I will not lay
One offering on thy shrine,
Though others their devotions pay
As though thou wert divine.

I love thee not. I know deceit
And guile are in thy heart,
That all thy words so soft and sweet,
Are tricks of woman's art.

I love thee not. The simplest mind
Is dearer far to me,
(Though far less brilliant and refined,)
Than ever thine can be!

SNOW-BALL.

VIBURNUM. *Class* 5. — *Order* 3.

Flowers in round clusters—white. Berries scarlet. A tall, graceful shrub.

Thoughts of Heaven.

'T is good
To be subdued at times; the heart is wooed
By these pure impulses to purer things.
Cherish within your souls whatever brings
Moments of sweet communion with high thought.
Joy hath its ministries, but griefs are fraught
With gentler blessings. Let them come, in soft
And tender eloquence, and bear aloft
Your faith on the white spirit-wings of prayer.

SNOWDROP.

GALANTHUS. *Class* 6. — *Order* 1.

Flowers white—the earliest that appear.

I am not a summer friend.

And dost thou think, thou foolish youth,
   That I shall say me '*Yea*'
To *any* fate, or *any* chains
   That bid me part from thee?

I will not. No, thy vow is here,
   Deep graven on my heart,
Which reads—'Come want, come shame, come death,
   We, dearest, ne'er will part!'

Hast thou forgotten it so soon?
   Then must I, too, believe
That what the proverb says is true,
   'Men promise, to deceive.'

No, dearest; I've a heart too strong
   To shrink from any strife,
Save that which would o'ermaster it
   Were I another's wife.

STAR OF BETHLEHEM.

ORNITHOGALUM. *Class* 6. — *Order* 1.

Root bulbous. Flowers white, six-petalled, with no calyx.

Let us follow Jesus.

SHALL we not follow where his feet have trod,
  And, by an humble love, and faith sincere,
Approach the likeness of the Son of God?
  His *Life* is with us, and his quickening *Word*—
Shall these be hidden from our daily sight,
  Or only 'neath the temple's arches heard,
Or dreamed of in the still, inactive night?
  Oh, no! His holy lessons shall be learned
By wayside connings in our daily walk;
  And, as the hearts of his disciples burned
When listening, as they journeyed, to his talk,
  So shall our hearts be thrilled, *our* souls subdued,
By the deep wisdom of his gentle speech,
  Until with light, and peace, and love imbued,
His kingdom, and its rest divine, we reach.

STRAWBERRY.

FRAGARIA. *Class* 12. — *Order* 13.

We have two native species of the Strawberry, which are capable of great improvement by cultivation. Flowers white.

Perfect Excellence.

UNTOUCHED by mortal passion,
 Thou seem'st of heavenly birth,
Pure as the effluence of a star
 Just reached our distant earth!

*

An inward light, to guide thee,
 Unto thy soul is given,
Pure and serene as its divine
 Original in heaven.
Type of the ransomed Psyche!
 How gladly, hand in hand,
To some new world I'd fly with thee
 From off this mortal strand.

J. ALDRICH.

SUMACH.

RHUS. *Class* 5. — *Order* 3.

Flowers greenish. Berries in cone-like clusters—bright red.

Splendid Misery.

OH, give me back my maiden haunt
  Beside the meadow brook;
I weary for the simple scenes
  My foolish heart forsook.
A couch beneath our cottage-roof
  Gave calm and sweet repose;
I never wakened then to weep,
  Nor slept to dream of woes.

Now dwell I here, a slave 'mid slaves—
  A kid within a fold;
Alas! I do not love my chains
  Although they are of gold.
I do not love these gaudy rooms,
  This incense-laden air;
How sweeter far the mountain-rocks
  And wild winds breathing there.

SUN-FLOWER.

HELIANTHUS. *Class* 19. — *Order* 3.

This plant grows eight or ten feet high. Leaves and flowers very large. Flowers yellow, and turn with the sun.

Smile on me still.

THE rose needs not the summer light,
The bird needs not the sheltering tree,
So much as I, in sorrow's night,
    Need smiles from thee.

Oh, never let thine eye grow cold,
Thy cherished voice grow rude to me;
But let thy lip, as oft of old,
    Still smile on me.

SWEET WILLIAM.

DIANTHUS BARBATUS. *Class* 10. — *Order* 2.

Root perennial. Flowers aggregate and brilliant.

Gallantry.

THE knights of old might envy thee
  Thy courtly grace of mien;
Thy noble daring, brave and free,
  In every dangerous scene.

To age how kind thy courtesy;
  To woman how sincere!
Alike removed from vanity,
  From artifice, and fear.

SYRINGA — CAROLINA.

PHILADELPHUS INODORUS. *Class* 12. — *Order* 1.

A native of the Southern States. Flowers white, large and scentless.

Memory.

OH, Memory! thou only wakener of the dead!
   Thou only treasurer of the vanished past!
How welcome art thou, when bright hope is fled,
   And sorrow's mantle o'er the soul is cast!
Back o'er those days, too beautiful to last,
   Thy gentle hand will lead the saddened thought;
And though the tears may trickle warm and fast,
   Yet thy sweet pictures with such peace are fraught,
     The heart, beguiled, exclaims, 'This is the fount I sought!'

THISTLE.

CARDUUS. *Class* 19. — *Order* 1.

Flowers large and purple. Whole plant very prickly.

Never forget.

Never forget the holy love
  It hath been ours to keep
Undimmed amid all toils and cares—
  The true, the pure, the deep.
The trusting love of early youth,
Still fair in its own changeless truth.

Never forget—it hath been joy,
  In suffering and in tears,
To know that thou wert still the same
  As in our earlier years.
The cup of life were bitterer yet,
Could I but deem thou wouldst forget.

MISS J. A. FLETCHER.

TULIP.

TULIPA. *Class* 6. — *Order* 1.

Corolla bell-shaped. No calyx. Color of the flower, in its natural state, crimson. By cultivation it has been made to assume every variety of hue.

Beautiful Eyes.

MELTING, dazzling, tender, bright,
Full of Love's own gentle light;
Now downcast, and now uplifted,
With a world of beauty gifted,
Drooping now with silent thought,
Now with joy and gladness fraught,
Arch and mirthful, soft and pensive,
Now assailing, now defensive—
Filled with glory from the skies—
Ah! who can describe thine eyes?

VERBENA.

VERBENA. *Class* 14. — *Order* 1.

This is a tall, slender plant, that requires training like a vine. Flowers pink or scarlet—in bright, beautiful clusters. Blossoms profusely.

Sensibility.

THINE eye at others' sorrow weeps,
  Thy lip at others' joy looks gay;
Thy heart's deep fount of feeling keeps
  In gentle, yet perpetual play.

The charms of nature thrill thy soul,
  For nature's own true child thou art;
And waves of earnest feeling roll
  In ceaseless music through thy heart.

VIOLET.

VIOLA. *Class* 5. — *Order* 1.

Flowers blue, white, yellow and tri-color. The blue Violet is most common in New England.

Faithfulness.

Oh, shame may come upon thy name,
   And want and suffering dim thine eye;
But thou wilt find me still the same—
   For love like mine can never die.

I will be thine through weal and wo,
   Through days of joy and sorrow's night;
My faith like morning's beams shall glow,
   My love shall be thy quenchless light.

VERNAL GRASS.

ANTHOXANTHUM. *Class* 3. — *Order* 2.

Native of Europe and India. Naturalized in America. Sweet-scented.

Poor but Happy.

MEN call us poor—it may be true
   Amid the gay and glittering crowd;
We feel it, though our wants are few,
   Yet envy not the proud.
The freshness of Love's early flowers,
   Heart-sheltered through long years of want,
Pure hopes and quiet joys are ours,
   That wealth could never grant.

W. H. BURLEIGH.

WALLFLOWER.

CHEIRANTHUS. *Class* 14. — *Order* 2.

This is a beautiful, fragrant flower, growing upon old walls, and among the ruins of castles and abbeys.

Fidelity in Misfortune.

AN emblem true thou art
 Of Love's enduring lustre, given
To cheer a lonely heart.

BARTON.

FLOWER of the solitary place!
 Gray Ruin's golden crown,
That lendest melancholy grace
 To haunts of old Renown:
Thou mantlest o'er the battlement,
 By strife or storm decayed;
And fillest up each envious rent
 Time's canker tooth hath made.

MOIR.

WATER LILY.

NYMPHÆ. *Class* 13. — *Order* 1.

Flowers white, with yellow germ and anthers. Very splendid, and deliciously fragrant.

Eloquence.

It welleth up from brimming founts
   Deep hidden in the soul—
And with a strong, resistless power
   Its chainless waters roll!
It gushes out in words of fire—
   It scorches with its breath—
And as the heart is pure or dark,
   Its words are life or death!

In Justice' great and outraged name,
   That giant voice doth crave
Redress for earth's down-trodden ones,
   And freedom for the slave!
And it has softer, gentler tones,
   To soothe the broken heart—
To bind its tender, bleeding wounds,
   And hope and peace impart

Miss C. A. FILLEBROWN.

WILLOW.

SALIX. *Class* 21. — *Order* 2.

There are many species of the Willow, most of which have beautiful, tassel-like blossoms, very odorous.

Forsaken.

I HAD a heart! I had a heart!
   'T was a gay and a happy thing;
And it danced about in my youthful breast
   Like a lamb in the flowery spring;
But now it lies like a slaughtered lamb,
   Its life-blood trickling out;
'T is a faithless heart to believe him false—
   I told him it should not doubt!—
     Doubt, doubt, doubt!
Oh, days pass on, long, weary days,
   But they bring no end to doubt!

WITCH HAZEL.

HAMAMELIS VIRGINICA. *Class* 4. — *Order* 2.

Indigenous to America. Flowers yellow. The divining-rods used by *money-diggers* to discover lost or hidden treasures, are made of the twigs of this shrub.

A Spell.

OUR *witches* are no longer old
And wrinkled beldames, Satan-sold,
But young and gay and laughing creatures,
With the heart's sunshine on their features;
Their sorcery—the light which dances
When the raised lid unveils its glances,
And the low-breathed and gentle tone,
   Faintly responding unto ours,
Soft, dream-like as a fairy's moan,
   Above its nightly-closing flowers.

J. G. WHITTIER.

WOODBINE.

LONICERA. *Class* 5. — *Order* 1.

There are many species of the Woodbine, all of which are luxuriant and beautiful.

Fraternal Love.

I THINK of thee, my sister,
   In my sad and lonely hours,
And the thought of thee comes o'er me
   Like the breath of morning flowers.
Like music that enchants the ear,
   Like sights that bless the eye,
Like the verdure of the meadow,
   The azure of the sky;
Like rainbow in the evening,
   Like blossom on the tree,
Is the thought of thee, dear sister,
   Is the tender thought of thee!

JOHN KENYON.

YARROW.

ACHILLEA. *Class* 19. — *Order* 11.

Flowers of a dull white. Rays yellowish. Medicinal.

A cure for the heart ache.

ART thou forsaken? Cold and dark, indeed,
  The fate unsoothed by sympathetic tears!
And well the stricken heart unstanched may bleed,
  With no soft, pitying voice to lull its fears.
'Look up, thou poor forsaken!' Jesus sped,
  All trustful, through a lot as dark as thine;
And know'st thou not that wheresoe'er he led,
  The path tends onward to a rest divine?
Art thou reviled? Do foes ensnare thy feet?
  Do proud ones mock thee, and thy friends betray?
Thou canst not drain the bitter from the sweet,
  Nor pluck the rose and throw the thorn away.
But, like thy Saviour, turn the other cheek
  When one is struck, and say, 'Thou art forgiven!'
Like him be faithful, and like him he meek,
  And speed, as he sped, hopefully to heaven!

ZINNIA.

Class 19. — *Order* 2.

Flowers red, purple and yellow. The large scarlet Zinnia is most beautiful.

I mourn your absence.

THE sun is bright—its golden rays
    Gild mountain-top and flower;
O'er rock, and wave, and vale it plays,
    From morn till evening hour.
But, ah! no beauty in its beams
    My weary heart can see,
While rocks, and vales, and glancing streams
    Keep me away from thee!

The waves to *others* wear a light
    More glorious than the sky;
To *me* earth's hues are only bright
    Reflected from thine eye.
The world may deem me dull and sad—
    I care not how that be;
I never can, nor will be glad,
    My love, away from thee!

INDEX OF FLOWERS.

Amaranth	Immortality
Anemone	Frailty
Aster	Beauty in Retirement
Acacia	Platonic Love
Apple-blossom	Fame speaks you great and good
Ash	Grandeur
Alyssum	Worth beyond Beauty
Bachelor's Button	Hope in Misery
Balm	Sweets of Social Intercourse
Balm of Gilead	I am cured
Balsam	Impatience
Barberry	Petulance
Bay Leaf	I change but in dying
Birch	Gracefulness
Bindweed	Humility
Blue bell	Constancy
Box	Stoicism
Broome	Neatness
Burdock	Importunity
Calla	Feminine Modesty
Chamomile	Energy in Adversity
Candytuft	Indifference
Cardinal Flower	Distinction
Carnation	Pride
Catchfly	A Snare
Cedar Tree	Spiritual Strength
Cherry-blossom	Spiritual Beauty
China Aster	Your sentiments meet with a return
Chrysanthemum	A heart left to desolation
Cinquefoil	Love, constant but hopeless
Clematis	Mental Excellence
Columbine	I cannot give thee up
Corn	Riches
Cowslip	Native Grace

Coreopsis	Always Cheerful
Coriander	Concealed Merit
Cypress	Disappointed Hopes
Dahlia	Elegance and Dignity
Daisy	Beauty and Innocence
Dandelion	Coquetry
Dew-plant	Serenade
Elder	Compassion
Eglantine	Poetry
Everlasting	Always remembered
Evergreen	Poverty and Worth
Fir	Time
Flowering Reed	Confidence in Heaven
Forget-me-not	True Love
Foxglove	I am not ambitious for myself, but for you
Fuchsia	Humble Love
Gentian	Virgin Pride

Geranium —
    Rose - Preference
    Scarlet - Thou art changed
    Oak - True Friendship
    Lemon - Tranquility of Mind
    Silver-leaved - Recall

Gilly Flower	Lasting Beauty
Golden Rod	Encouragement
Grape	Charity
Grass	Submission
Hawthorn	Hope
Hazel	Reconciliation
Heliotrope	Devotion
Hibiscus	Beauty is vain
Hollyhock	Ambition
Honeysuckle	Fidelity
Hop	Injustice

Houstonia	Quiet Happiness
Hydrangea	Heartlessness
Ice-plant	Your looks freeze me
Iris	A Message
Ivy	I have found one true heart
Jasmine	Amiability
Jonquil	Affection returned
King-cup	I wish I was rich
Laburnum	Pensive Beauty
Lady's Slipper	Capricious Beauty
Larkspur	Inconstancy
Laurel	Virtue is true Beauty
Lavender	Acknowledgement
Lemon	Discretion
Lettuce	Cold-hearted
Lilac	First Emotion of Love
Lily	Purity
Lily of the Valley	Heart withering in secret
Locust	Affection beyond the grave
Lupine	Dejection
London Pride	Frivolity
Mallows	Sweet Disposition
Maple	Reserve
Marygold	Contempt
Mignonette	Moral Beauty
Mimosa	Sensitiveness
Moss	Maternal Love
Myrtle	Love in Absence
Nasturtion	Patriotism
Nightshade	Dark Thoughts
Oak	Hospitality
Oleander	Beware!
Orange Flowers	Woman's Worth
Pansy	Tender and pleasant Thoughts

Passion Flower	Religious Fervor
Pea, Everlasting	Wilt thou go?
Pea, Sweet	Departure
Peach-blossom	I am your captive
Petunia	Thou art less proud than they deem thee
Peony	Ostentation
Phlox	Our souls are united
Pine	Time and Faith
Pink	White, Lovely and pure Affection
Pink	Red, Woman's Love
Polyanthus	Confidence
Potato	Beneficence
Poppy	Forgetfulness
Primrose	Modest Worth
Primrose, Evening	I am more faithful than thou
Rose-bud	Confession of Love
Rose, Bridal	Happy Love
Rose, Burgundy	Simplicity and Beauty
Rose, Damask	Bashful Love
Rose, Moss	Superior Merit
Rose, Multiflora	Grace
Rose, White	Too young to love
Rose, Red-leaved	Diffidence
Sage	Domestic Virtues
Snapdragon	Dazzling, but dangerous
Snowball	Thoughts of Heaven
Snowdrop	I am not a summer friend
Star of Bethlehem	Let us follow Jesus
Strawberry	Perfect Eellence
Sumach	Splendid Misery
Sunflower	Smile on me still
Sweet William	Gallantry
Syringa	Memory
Thistle	Never forget

Tulip	Beautiful Eyes
Verbena	Sensibility
Violet	Faithfulness
Vernal Grass	Poor, but Happy
Wallflower	Fidelity in Misfortune
Water Lily	Eloquence
Willow	Forsaken
Witch Hazel	A Spell
Woodbine	Fraternal Love
Yarrow	A cure for the heart ache
Zinnia	I mourn your absence

Suggested Reading

de Latour, Charlotte. Le Langage Des Fleurs. 1819. Garnier, 1856.

Delachênaye, B. Abécédaire de Flore Ou Langage Des Fleurs. Paris, de l'imprimerie de P. Didot l'Ainé, 1811.

Ingram, John Henry. Flora Symbolica . F. W. Warne and Co., 1869.

Laufer, Geraldine Adamich. Tussie-Mussies: The Language of Flowers. Workman Pub., 1993.

Mayo, Sarah C. Edgarton. Fables of Flora. Powers and Straw, 1844.

---. The Floral Fortune-Teller. 1846. A. Tompkins, 1855.

Phillips, Henry. Floral Emblems. Saunders and Otley, 1825.

Rafinesque, Constantine Samuel. Medical Flora. Atkinson & Alexander, 1828.

Seaton, Beverly. The Language of Flowers : A History. University Press of Virginia, 1995.

Shoberl, Frederic. The Language of Flowers with Illustrative Poetry. 1835. Lea and Blanchard, 1843.

Wirt, Elizabeth Washington Gamble. Flora's Dictionary. 1829. Fielding Lucas Jr., 1832.

www.ingramcontent.com/pod-product-compliance
Lightning Source LLC
Chambersburg PA
CBHW022115040426
42450CB00006B/706